Blood, Sweat and Glorious Thundering Fifties
The Combined Volume

By

Mike Woodhouse

This book is dedicated to all those I've had the pleasure of working with during my railway career, and those who have taken on this work in the preservation movement. While often your blood and sweat to keep these vehicles in service goes unseen, the product of your labours is appreciated.

Cover Photo: A line up of class 50s on the depot at Plymouth Laira. Photo: Rail Photoprints
Rear Cover Photo Top: Mike with 50017 on the Plym Valley Railway June 2013. Photo: Ted Reading
Rear Cover Photo Bottom: Mike in the doorway of Laira's 'flagship' 50007 Sir Edward Elgar at Waterloo about to set off for Carlisle 11th April 1992. Photo Chris Lunn – Mike Woodhouse Collection

ISBN 978-1-8384369-2-6

Contents

Combined Volume Foreword 3
New Fifties **5**
Vulcan—Crewe From The Beginning 6
Cement to Cornwall 10
Fire Fire Fire 11
Leg Out of Bed 11
Rodder's Knock 12
Razor Blades to Razor Blades 13
The Last Rites of Valiant and Thunderer 14
End of the Line at Crewe 15
Discover During COVID-19 15
Blood Sweat and Fifties **16**
D400 Comes to Plymouth 16
Westerns Loose Out to Hoovers 17
Headcode Matter 18
Nameplates Ahoy! 19
Hercules III 20
50040's Double Life 21
Dawn of a New Image 21
Why 50149? 22
A Winter's Tale 22
Hard Day's Night 25
Men of the Greyhounds 27
Waterloo Sunset 27
Ups and Downs, Western Style 28
Day Return to Penzance 29
Mishaps with the Milk 30
A Busman's Day Out 32
The Road to the Scilly Isles 33
Thundering Fifties **34**
Introduction and Foreword 34
First and Last 35
Summer Working: Exeter 1985 36
Silent Night 37
The Lifting Road 38
'F' Exam Programme 39
Friday Rendezvous 41
Shap Here We Come! 43
Thunderer's Last Exam 46
'The Minster Marauder' 47
Hope and Glory 50
The Road to the Cutter's Torch 54
Class 50s as at December 1993 and Now 57
Past Times by Andy Griffiths 58
Woodhouse Wanderings: 1: Mid-Hants Railway 59
2: Torbay and Dartmouth 61
3: The East Lancashire Railway 62
4: Bodmin and Wentford Railway 65
Project Defiance 66
Glorious Fifties **69**
Introduction and Preface 69
School Boy's Surprise—Summer 1958 69
50019 Off the Road: A Diary of Events 70
Fury with 'Furious' 50034 at Old Oak Common 1979 72
The Bishops Triple 73
Summertime Special: National Railway Museum 1993 75
Project Defiance 50149: Judgement Day—18th August 1993 76
Val's Curtain Call 77
Geoff's Dream 79
Glorious—Against All Odds 81
The Finale of 50s on British Rail 84
Workings: Class 50 Mileages 1992-1994 90
Further Woodhouse Wanderings: 1: Bodmin and Wenford Railway 91
2: North York Moors Railway 92
3: Plym Valley Railway 93
In Conclusion 95
The Fifty Fund **96**

Foreword—Geoff Hudson

When Mike described maintaining Class 50s as Blood Sweat & Fifties, he was conveying an image of the arduous work, heavy engineering, and the often challenging task of keeping these charismatic locomotives in service.

However, there is another side to the challenges presented in maintaining them that is often over-looked and rarely told. That is the managerial responsibility for the overall operation and maintenance of the fifty fleet.

As Area Fleet Manager Plymouth based at Laira Depot it was my responsibility to manage the fleet in the final years of Class 50 operation on British Rail. This proved to be quite a daunting task for several reasons.

Firstly, their Home Depot was not actually on the route between Exeter and Waterloo but fifty miles west of Exeter in Plymouth. This in effect meant that their operational sphere was remote from the depot. This situation was further compounded by the depot at the other end, adjacent to Waterloo (Stewarts Lane), had extremely limited facilities for Class 50 maintenance. So any locomotives requiring significant attention near London, would have to travel across the capital to Old Oak Common. Consequently when a loco left Laira it was out for a minimum of two days, if not more, and therefore had to be basically self sufficient.

The Waterloo Exeter route has a demanding duty cycle, with many stops, followed by high speed running, and west of Salisbury much of the route is single track in remote countryside. Any locomotive failure there would quickly result in a lengthy delay not only to that train but also to services in the opposite direction. To help counter these prob-lems, I appointed two Technical Riding Inspectors to cover the route principally between Exeter and Salisbury. This proved a remarkable success as a driver on an ailing Class 50 knew he was not alone, and help was out there. This encouraged them to keep going and the travelling inspectors would use ingenious means to meet up with the 'patient' and diagnose the problem and hopefully affect a repair, or at least a temporary fix to get out of trouble.

In 1989 when I was appointed as Area Fleet Man-ager, BR was in the throes of Sectorisation, and the run up to privatisation with all the uncertainty for the staff that this entailed. Laira was designated an InterCity Depot with principal role for HST Ser-vices on the Great Western mainline, but it was not as straightforward as that, as we had six customers all demanding our time: namely Great Western and Cross Country HSTs, Network SouthEast Waterloo Exeter Class 50s, Regional Railways local Devon and Cornwall Services, Railfreight Distribution China Clay Services and finally Civil Engineer's

Laira's Flagship, a Very Special Locomotive; 50007 'Sir Edward Elgar', passes Tisbury with the 08.10 Exeter St. Davids to London Waterloo on a misty 30th March 1991. Photo: Geoff Cann

Class 50s. All of these placed conflicting demands on the depot and the Class 50s consumed a lot of our resources.

With the rundown and ever diminishing fleet size supply of overhauled spares became a real problem, particularly Power Units and Main Generators and those followers of the class will realise that a shortage of these critical components had a significant impact on availability. In addition, Main Generator failure often coupled with sympathetic Traction Motor Flashover would result in lengthy delays for replacement parts and then competing for space on the Jack Road. Every effort was made to keep them going and only locomotives with the lowest mileage and engine hours were selected for duty on the Waterloo – Exeter's. British Rail's long

not only gave followers another 2 years of service but allowed us to put together an extended farewell programme to see them off in style. It also had a completely unplanned benefit that ultimately helped the preservation groups, as it meant the class were still registered as an operational fleet with British Rail right up to the end on the 31st March 1994. So when the privatised railway commenced on the 1st April Class 50 was a designated locomotive class and this subsequently made it a lot easier for their new owners to return Fifties to the mainline.

All of the above would not have been possible without the dedication and commitment of the whole team at Laira who rose to the challenge, and despite shortages of materials and limited funds being available for the overhaul of spare parts, managed to extend the Class 50's service life to the date of Rail Privatisation. This was undertaken at a time of great uncertainty when they also had a heavy workload for our InterCity customer. But such was the pride that

The Pride of Laira: 50033 'Glorious', wonderfully prepared for a life in the hands of National Railway Museum with some of the depot staff and apprentices who worked to bring the locomotive up to the high standard for presentation. Photo: Paul Furtek

term traction for the Waterloo Exeter service was the Class 159 DMU, but towards the very end of loco hauled trains on the route, surplus Class 47/7s were drafted in at Old Oak Common. However, they struggled on the route with Brake Blocks wearing out rapidly and with the large number and frequent station stops, the Class 50s with their superior acceleration proved better able to keep time. As withdrawals gained pace interest in the class increased markedly and we decided that all future railtours would have locos presented to the highest possible standard, and as you will see Mike explains some of the behind scene action. The final date for operation of the class was May 1992 but such was the following Network Southeast agreed to keep the last three remaining locos for railtour use. A complete and unplanned decision, but this

the 'Girls' as they became known were always turned out in immaculate condition and performed faultlessly in their final two years.

This achievement is tribute to their professionalism and dedication, and I am proud to have worked with and lead such a magnificent Team.

To have been associated with the operation of Class 50s has been a real and enjoyable privilege and a way of life not repeated on today's railway. Mike's books have long been out of print and this combined volume will be eagerly awaited by Class 50 supporters and for those of us who were there, a reminder of those wonderful if sometimes demanding times.

Geoff Hudson
Area Fleet Manager
Laira Depot Plymouth - 1989 to 1996

New Fifties

It is still amazing to me that over twenty five years after the withdrawal of class 50s from service with British Rail, how much interest there is in class 50 preservation.

My old depot; 83D/84A/LA, Plymouth Laira, has given the biggest fleet of locomotives into the preservation movement; through the 60s with steam locomotives like saddle tank 1363, to some of the High Speed Train power cars just sold (in 2021) .

Even after 20 years of retirement, requests still come in asking if there are anymore class 50 stories from the workshop floor. So during the COVID-19 lockdown my mind turned to see what more could be retold.

This new combined book is the result of that activity: the stories first published in the long sold out, Blood Sweat and Fifties, Thundering Fifties, and Glorious Fifties have been updated, along with new stories, new photographs and some additional insights. Hopefully this will be an enjoyable read. Your purchase of this new book will provide a direct contribution towards keeping the class 50 locomotives maintained and operated by the Class 50 Alliance (supported by The Fifty Fund) in operation and active on the UK rail network.

Mike Woodhouse
Ivybridge,
Devon
—November 2021

Mike with the nameplate from the withdrawn 50014. Photo: Mike Woodhouse Collection

A line up of preserved 50s at the Old Oak Common Open Day 2nd September 2017. Of the 50 built in the late 1960s, 18 are now in the hands of different preservation groups. Photo: Dave Redbourne

Vulcan - Crewe From the Beginning

Using the British Rail headcode 0Z00 Vulcan Works to Crewe Works the following here are the delivery notes from 1967 and the traffic reports.

Once an inspection had been carried out British Rail and English Electric tested the brand new D4XX locomotives, they were put onto a loaded trial run and return, with fourteen Bogies. The British Rail headcode being 1T60 Crewe Works to Carlisle in which they had a climb of Shap summit on the outward leg. The train then returned south sometimes via the Settle and Carlisle route after running around at Carlisle. All faults noted would be rectified by English Electric before entering rail traffic.

D400 passed through the gates of the Vulcan Foundry works for the first time onto British Rail metals on 4 September as 0Z00 light engine trip to Chester and return. It re-emerged on 20 September as the 6T63 Farington Junction yard - Carlisle with a test run of concrete sleepers routed via the S and C route.

On 23 September D400 worked 0Z00 light engine from Vulcan Foundry to Crewe Works but it was

D435 (later 50035 'Ark Royal') hurries through Oxenholme with 1T60 a Crewe - Carlisle test train, 31st July 1968. Photo: Derek Cross – Rail Photoprints

returned the very next day, 24 September, for rectifications.

The locomotive was finally accepted by British Rail on 3 October at Crewe Works after one month of test running under the English Electric Company supervision. From here on the commissioning team provided week ending traffic reports until the final delivery of D449 on 11th December 1968.

The traffic reports, week endings and the delivery dates to British Rail are as follows:

TRAFFIC REPORT WEEK ENDING 21 OCTOBER 1967

D400	0Z00	6 October 1967 Vulcan Works – Crewe
D400	IT60	17 October 1967. 15 bogies ETH. Loaded trial run Crewe – Carlisle via S & C.
D400	-	Driver training.
D401	IT60	Commissioning trials.

TRAFFIC REPORT WEEK ENDING 19 NOVEMBER 1967

D400	-	Crewe Driver training.
D401	0Z00	Vulcan Works for investigation.
D402	0Z00	Vulcan Works - Crewe Works for commissioning.
D403	0Z00	Vulcan Works - Crewe Works for commissioning.

TRAFFIC REPORT WEEK ENDING 26 JANUARY 1968

D402	-	Driver training Polmadie - Dumfries.
D404	-	Driver training Perth - Stirling.

TRAFFIC REPORT WEEK ENDING 2 FEBRUARY 1968

D402	-	Driver training Polmadie.
D404	-	Driver training Perth.
D400, D404, D405		Perth - Crewe Night sleeper duties.
D404	-	29 January 1968 departed 21.15hrs for Crewe - Night sleeper, arrived back at 04.36hrs from Crewe. 1 February 1968 departed once again from Perth at 22.35hrs for Crewe after being utilised on two return trips Perth - Stirling on 30 January 1968.
D400	-	Arrived at Perth at 06.40hrs - 30 January 1968 and two return trips Perth - Stirling it departed 22.35hrs for Crewe 30 January.
D405	-	Arrived Perth 09.30hrs 29 January 1968 departed Perth 22.35hrs on evening 29 January 1968 and arrived at 04.36hrs on 31 January 1968 with two return trips Perth – Stirling on 31 January 1968 departed Perth 22.35hrs 31 January 1968 and arrived 04.36hrs on 2nd February 1968 with two trips Perth - Stirling and depart Perth 22.35hrs February 1968.

TRAFFIC REPORT WEEK ENDING 10 FEBRUARY 1968

D402	-	Driver training duties – Polmadie
D400, D403, D404		Crewe - Perth night sleeper duties and return.
D406	-	Derby on wheel slip trials.

TRAFFIC REPORT WEEK ENDING 17 FEBRUARY 1968
D402, D404   -   Driver training duties Polmadie.
D400, D401, D403   Crewe - Perth night duty sleepers and return.

TRAFFIC REPORT WEEK ENDING 24 FEBRUARY 1968— As per 17 February 1968 plus.
D410   0Z00   Vulcan Works - Crewe Works Arrived 13.00hrs 23 February 1968.

TRAFFIC REPORT WEEK ENDING 2 MARCH 1968
D400-D406, D410, D412   In traffic
D406   0Z00   Crewe Works - Vulcan Works for Modifications 26 February 1968.
D412   0Z00   Vulcan Works - Crewe Works 27 February 1968.

TRAFFIC REPORT WEEK ENDING 9 MARCH 1968
D400-D404, D410,D412   Passenger and freightliner, driver training duties within the Scottish Region.
D413   0Z00   Vulcan Works - Crewe Works 7 March 1968.

TRAFFIC REPORT WEEK ENDING 16 MARCH 1968
D400-D405, D407, D410, D421 D413
                               Crewe - Glasgow - Perth.

TRAFFIC REPORT WEEK ENDING 23 MARCH 1968
D400-D405, D407-D413   In traffic.
D409   0Z00   Vulcan Works - Crewe Works 19 March 1968.
D411   0Z00   Vulcan Works - Crewe Works 20 March 1968.
D408   0Z00   Vulcan Works - Crewe Works 22 March 1968.

TRAFFIC REPORT WEEK ENDING 30 MARCH 1968
D400-D413   -   In traffic.
D400   -   To the Vulcan Works from Preston 29 March 1968.
D406   -   To Preston from Vulcan Works 29 March 1968.

TRAFFIC REPORT WEEK ENDING 6 APRIL1968
D406   -   Driver training Preston Lostock Hall Depot.
D400-D413   -   In traffic.
D415, D417   0Z00   Vulcan Works - Crewe Works 2 April 1968.

TRAFFIC REPORT WEEK ENDING 13 APRIL 1968
D400-D413, D415, D417   In traffic.
D400   -   Under modification at Vulcan Works.
D410   -   On the load bank test bed at Toton it was returned to Crewe 9 April 1968 and hauled
                                11.25hrs Crewe - Windermere without incident back into normal traffic on the 23.09hrs
                                Freightliner service Crewe – Glasgow 9 April 1968.
D405   -   On high speed 100mph train trials Edinburgh - Glasgow 7 April 1968.

TRAFFIC REPORT WEEK ENDING 20 APRIL 1968
D400-D418   -   In traffic.
D404   -   Driver training Carlisle - Upperby.

TRAFFIC REPORT WEEK ENDING 27 APRIL 1968
D400-D418   -   In traffic
D419   -   At Carlisle Kingmoor under investigation 27 April 1968.
D414   0Z00   Vulcan Works - Crewe Works 23 April 1968.
D419   0Z00   Vulcan Works - Crewe Works 24 April 1968.
D416   0Z00   Vulcan Works - Crewe Works 25 April 1968.

TRAFFIC REPORT WEEK ENDING 4 MAY 1968
D400-D421   -   In traffic
D420   0Z00   Vulcan Works - Crewe Works 29 April 1968.
D421   0Z00   Vulcan Works - Crewe Works 2 May 1968.
D409   -   Unable to attain high speed for High speed running test by the Civil Engineer: three
                                coaches and one dynamometer car 30 April 1968.

TRAFFIC REPORT WEEK ENDING 10 MAY 1968
D400-D423   -   In traffic.
D413   -   Driver training Carlisle – Upperby
D408   -   Failed IM46 north of Carlisle reason unknown 7 May 1968.
D422   0Z00   Vulcan Works - Crewe Works 7 May 1968.
D423   0Z00   Vulcan Works - Crewe Works 10 May 1968.

D426 and 439, both showing 0Z00 headcodes stand either side of D404 which just operated, or is just about to operate 1P16. The trio are captured on the fueling point at Crewe TMD in November 1970. The outer two locomotives have probably just returned from the Vulcan Foundry. Photo: Rail Photoprints

TRAFFIC REPORT WEEK ENDING 18 MAY 1968
| D400-D423 | - | In traffic. |

TRAFFIC REPORT WEEK ENDING 25 MAY 1968
D400-D424	-	In traffic.
D424	0Z00	Vulcan Works - Crewe Works 21 May 1968. Entered traffic after trials 00.17hrs Crewe
-		Perth 22 May 1968.
D401	-	At Crewe Works for derailment damage.
D403	0Z00	Transferred to Vulcan Works for modifications.

TRAFFIC REPORT WEEK ENDING 1 JUNE 1968.
| D400-D424 | - | In traffic. |
| D401 | - | Re-entered traffic ex Crewe Works after derailment damage on 29 May 1968. |

TRAFFIC REPORT WEEK ENDING 8 JUNE 1968.
D400-D425	-	In traffic.
D425	0Z00	Vulcan Works - Crewe Works 5 June 1968.
D401	0Z00	Crewe Works - Vulcan Works for modification 5 June 1968.

TRAFFIC REPORT WEEK ENDING 15 JUNE 1968
D400-D427	-	In traffic.
D427	0Z00	Vulcan Works - Crewe Works 10 June 1968.
D426	0Z00	Vulcan Works - Crewe Works 15 June 1968.

TRAFFIC REPORT WEEK ENDING 22 JUNE 1968
D400-D429	-	In traffic.
D428	0Z00	Vulcan Works - Crewe Works 18 June 1968.
D429	0Z00	Vulcan Works - Crewe Works 21 June 1968.

TRAFFIC REPORT WEEK ENDING 29 JUNE 1968
| D400-D430 | - | In traffic. |
| D430 | 0Z00 | Vulcan Works - Crewe Works 28 June 1968. |

TRAFFIC REPORT WEEK ENDING 6 JULY 1968
D400-D431   -   In traffic.
D431   0Z00   Vulcan Works - Crewe Works 1 July 1968.

TRAFFIC REPORT WEEK ENDING 13 JULY 1968
D400-D432   -   In traffic.
D432   0Z00   Vulcan Works - Crewe Works 12 July 1968.
D400   -   Tyre turning at Tyseley.6 July - 11 July 1968.

TRAFFIC REPORT WEEK ENDING 20 JULY 1968
D400-D433   -   In traffic.
D433   0Z00   Vulcan Works - Crewe Works 20 July 1968

TRAFFIC REPORT WEEK ENDING 27 JULY 1968
D400-D434   -   In traffic.
D434   0Z00   Vulcan Works - Crewe Works 23 July 1968.

TRAFFIC REPORT WEEK ENDING 3 AUGUST 1968
D400-D435   -   In traffic.
D435   0Z00   Vulcan Works - Crewe Works 1 August 1968.

TRAFFIC REPORT WEEK ENDING 17 AUGUST 1968
D400-D436   -   In traffic.
D436   0Z00   Vulcan Works - Crewe Works 14 August 1968.

TRAFFIC REPORT WEEK ENDING 14 SEPTEMBER 1968
D400-D439   -   In traffic.
D439   0Z00   Vulcan Works - Crewe Works 9 September 1968.

TRAFFIC REPORT WEEK ENDING 28 SEPTEMBER 1968
D400-D440   -   In traffic.
D438   0Z00   Vulcan Works - Crewe Works 16 September 1968.
D437   0Z00   Vulcan Works - Crewe Works 24 September 1968.
D440   0Z00   Vulcan Works - Crewe Works 25 September 1968.

TRAFFIC REPORT WEEK ENDING 5 OCTOBER 1968
D400-D443   -   In traffic.
D441   0Z00   Vulcan Works - Crewe Works 4 October 1968.
D443   0Z00   Vulcan Works - Crewe Works 4 October 1968.
D442   0Z00   Vulcan Works - Crewe Works 30 October 1968.

TRAFFIC REPORT WEEK ENDING 19 OCTOBER 1968
D400-D444   -   In traffic.
D444   0Z00   Vulcan Works - Crewe Works 14 October 1968.

TRAFFIC REPORT WEEK ENDING 26 OCTOBER 1968
D400-D445   -   In traffic.
D445   0Z00   Vulcan Works - Crewe Works 21 October 1968.

TRAFFIC REPORT WEEK ENDING 2 NOVEMBER 1968
D400-D446   -   In traffic.
D446   0Z00   Vulcan Works - Crewe Works 30 October 1968.

TRAFFIC REPORT WEEK ENDING 9 NOVEMBER 1968
D400-D447   -   In traffic.
D447   0Z00   Vulcan Works - Crewe Works 5 November 1968.

TRAFFIC REPORT WEEK ENDING 23 NOVEMBER 1968
D400-D448   -   In traffic.
D448   0Z00   Vulcan Works - Crewe Works 15 November 1968.

TRAFFIC REPORT WEEK ENDING 14 DECEMBER 1968
D400-D449   -   In traffic.
D449   0Z00   Vulcan Works - Crewe Works 11 December 1968.

After the last delivery in December 1968, it appears that the 0Z00 headcode continued to be used for transfers and test runs from The Vulcan Foundry to Crewe Traction Maintenance Depot into the 1970s.

Cement to Cornwall

In 1981 powder cement to Cornwall for the building industry came from the Blue Circle Cement Works at Westbury Wiltshire, it was trunked down to Plymouth Friary yard where the train split, with many workings being hauled by class fifties.

The first part was tripped by the Class 08, Laira's diesel electric shunter. The 0-6-0 hauled the wagons from Friary Yard to Plymstock Blue Circle works on the southern side of the River Plym overlooking Laira Depot.

At this time the train working was on a daily basis, changed from a once a week diagram.

The second half of the train went on a Plymouth Friary Yard - Chacewater diagram usually with a local work class fifty at 45 mph.

This train in the early days was formed of the familiar bauxite liveried Presflo`s which were changed over to the PCA tanks of the grey with Blue Circle markings in 1983.

The former train was classed as a Class 7 Freight 7B41, later changed to Class 6 6B41 as the wagon type speed increased from 45mph to 60mph.

This was a lovely turn to have a run out on if a class fifty was on test.

After booking on for the early turn at Laira 06.30 - 14.30hrs and given the job to ride with a class fifty on the Chacewater Cement was special mainly because nobody knew how long it would last due to its Cornish location. This being a booked time of 07.30hrs ex Friary Yard for an idyllic journey into Cornwall with the loaded cement train crossing over the Royal Albert Bridge in the early morning was always a delight looking over the River Tamar. On reaching Chacewater the class fifty would do the shunt and reform the returning empties. By midday the train was ready to leave the Chacewater sidings but headed west down to Drump Lane, Redruth to enable the locomotive to run around its train and the guard to change over the tail lamp. Once the signalman was notified this had been completed, the road was set for the class fifty to power up through the crossover and climb out onto the up mainline, heading East back to Plymouth Friary. This train formed the 13.45hrs ex St Blazey Yard-Plymouth Friary with any pick-up freight for any onward despatch.

We would run back to Laira from Plymouth Friary yard around 16.00hrs light engine, which meant a couple of hour's overtime.

The second part of the returning cement train empties came to Friary Yard with the Class 08 pilot later that afternoon for an evening departure to Westbury.

This leisurely turn was often worked by classes 25, 37, 47 and 50`s, the latter usually being on test or restricted to local workings only.

**50037 approaches Par with the Tavistock Junction - St. Blazey engineers service on 29th June 1979.
Photo: Rail Photoprints**

Fire Fire Fire

I was on the night shift at Laira in the late summer of 1991. The shift was nearly over the sky was getting light when I was approached by my shift supervisor. Control at Swindon, who look after all movements and maintenance on BR's Western Region, had rung through with a message; 50046 'Ajax' was on fire at Chippenham Station — the seat of the fire was thought to be the main generator. 50046 had been working the Up Night Riviera service which is the Monday to Friday 21.35 Penzance – London Paddington Sleeper (1A07), when it lost all power after Bath. The driver coasted the train into Chippenham Station where all the emergency services were alerted and the blaze attended to by the Wiltshire Fire Service.

Following the fire, 50046 was despatched from 81A, Old Oak Common, depot in West London to Laira for attention. That Friday evening I was back on shift at 22.30hrs, and found 'Ajax' berthed against the stop blocks on No2 Road waiting for the investigation, report writing and a decision on its future. During that shift, out of interest, I took it upon myself to see the impact of the fire on the locomotive's components. Armed with my torch I entered the engine room from the No 2 end cab. It was very dark with the acrid smell of burnt mica insulation which was almost overpowering. I shone my torch around and into the open commutator servicing hatches of the main generator. Whow! What a sight! Half the copper segments on the commutator were missing. These had melted in the extremely high temperatures and were now a large single solid block at the bottom dead centre of the generator housing. Here the liquid metal had flowed, drawn by gravity, and then cooled into a solid mass. The heat of the fire had also caused the windings to expand. Under this pressure their bandings and soldered joints had failed causing the assembly to burst open, and now they were splayed out in all directions looking like a rather dangerous hedgehog.

The main generator (serial number YA511P) had clearly been destroyed by the fire. It had been coupled to diesel power unit IH6846 and fitted into 50046 'Ajax', at Laira, only just over a year before. By the time of the fire, only 6007 engine hours had been recorded, which was about half the expected life for such parts after an overhaul.

Clearly the decision was taken that 50046 would continue, as in the Autumn of 1991, the locomotive was fitted with an overhauled power unit (IH6966) and main generator. This was one of the last overhauled/rebuilt by British Rail Engineering Ltd Crewe for Laira. However this combination of components did not last long, as three months later 50046 gave up this diesel set, and main generator to its sister class 50 locomotive, 50007 'Sir Edward Elgar' in early 1992. Both bogies (serial numbers No3 and No4) also swapped with those from under 50007. 50046 therefore became a hulk and shortly afterwards moved to MC Metals in Glasgow for Breaking: 'Farewell Old Fire Friend'.

I'm pleased to report that both cabs from 50046 'Ajax' did survive. One now resides on a Cornish farm after being purchased from Dave Cunningham who had based it along with his locomotive 50017 'Royal Oak' on the Ply Valley Railway 'The Woodland Line'. This No 1 end cab has been externally painted in BR Blue, and cosmetically restored internally. The No 2 end cab was transported to its new owner in Wellington (Shropshire) on 25th November 2009. The cab is reportedly in good order and mostly complete.

Leg Out of Bed

The term 'Leg Out of Bed' in mechanical engineering terms is used when an internal combustion engine's piston and connecting rod (or con-rod) part company at high speed. Usually this results in the con-rod trashing around until it breaks through the crankcase casting to the world outside. Usually at this point the power unit is a write off as the costs to affect a reliable repair are very high.

During my time on British Railways Western Region I have witnessed just about all types of traction, with both hydraulic and electric transmissions and DMUs exhibit this type of failure.

As the loss of a major component like a power unit will have a big economic and possibly a significant fleet availability impact, investigations always take place following a 'leg out of bed' to try and understand the causes, learn lessons and improve the care and maintenance procedures and processes.

The class 50 power unit, the English Electric 16CSVT*, suffered this fate several times during the 1980s and 90s. No less than eight units were written off this way causing a shortage over this period. However a rescue plan for four units was affected using Class 40 crankcases and engine blocks.

This was possible as the class 40 power unit was an English Electric 16SVT (an earlier development of what went on to be the 16CSVT) and used many of the same components as the unit fitted in a 50. These rebuilds mainly took place at Doncaster.

One oddity was that of a class 56 crankcase and block that was used to rebuild a class 50 power unit which fitted to 50010 by Doncaster Works.

* 16=no. of cylinders, C=Charge cooled, S=Supercharged - turbocharged in this case, V=V form, T=rail Traction use.

Below is a table of power units that were affected:

Crankcase No	Loco fitted to when new	Year of modification	Loco fitted to after rebuild	Notes	Loco fitted to at withdrawal
IH6933	D446	1984	50027	Class 40 Crankcase	50027
IH6934	D407	1984	50004	Scrapped	50002
iH6940	D412	1984	50003	Class 40 Crankcase	50020
IH6964	D436	1985	50047	Badly Damaged - Rebuilt	50047
IH5567	DP2/D400	1990	50037	Scrapped	50037
IH6960	D429	1990	50038	Scrapped	50038
IH6951	D423	1990	50032	Class 40 Crankcase	50029
IH6973	Spare	1984	50024	Class 56 Crankcase	50010

Sadly most of these rebuilds went for scrap. Including IH5567 which had started life in the prototype DP2. IH6933 is still in a serviceable class 50, as the prime mover in 50027 'Lion' which can be enjoyed on the Mid-Hants Railway.

Rodder's Knock

In 1978, not long before Class 50, 50021 was named 'Rodney' the locomotive came to grief with a Catastrophic failure of power unit IH6949. The piston had parted company from the con-rod. This was the first such failure of a English Electric 16CSVT on the Western Region and a new experience for the team at Laira.

Laira was asked to see if it could carry out the repair without 50021 going to main works at Doncaster. As The Plant was already full of 50s under repair or waiting for attention, and sending it there would just leave it out of traffic for a long time. Following discussions and agreements on funding, processes and ensuring we had the right tooling, the go ahead was given.

From our records we knew that this diesel set had originally been fitted to D419 and after an overhaul it had been transferred to D421 on 14th April 1970, so had given 11 years service in total, and 8 since the last major attention.

I was personally involved from the very start of this repair together with a colleague who had significant experience on English Electric power units from his five years working on locomotives built for and operated by East African railways (Class 87s with 12CSVTs). We started by stripping out all the smashed engine parts, and removed as much of the remaining oil and water as we could. At this point we noticed an internal casting fracture which was

The view through a 16CSVT crankcase door of IH6931, looking at the con-rod of piston B2 and the crankshaft. Piston A2's connecting rod can be seen above the shiny machined surface of the crank shaft as it is being lowered into position.
Photo: Joseph Burr

promptly reported back to management.

It was suggested by an ex-Royal Navy member of staff at Laira that perhaps the specialists at Devonport Dockyard, the other side of the city, could help. Contact was made and two of their staff joined the early shift the following day so see the damage first hand, and help work out what type of fix could be achieved.

Over the next three days the combined Laira and Devonport team came to the conclusion that the best chance of affecting a repair was to drill, and stitch the fracture, and then fill any gaps with two part metal epoxy resin. This was duly carried out by the dockyard who had the facilities. The question that remained was would the repair hold and for how long under operating pressures and temperatures.

IH6949 was left to cure for three days by which time a new cylinder liner, piston and con-rod had been delivered from Doncaster Works.

During the next week or so we re-assembled 50021's power unit then filled the coolant system with untreated water. After a short wait to let the water settle, we inspected the inside of the crankcase and with some relief we found that no water was weeping through the repaired parts.

We then emptied the water out and refilled the coolant system with the usual combination of water and antifreeze. We then checked again and fortunately the power unit was still water tight.

There are two primary reasons for the two stage test of the coolant system. The first one is purely economic, 133 gallons of antifreeze treated water costs money and if a leak was substantial, that coolant would be flowing into the sump from where it would have to be disposed of as it couldn't be reused. The second reason is technical, the antifreeze changes the properties of the water allowing it to flow through smaller gaps than plain water alone. Testing in this order saves waste and ensures the system is fully sealed.

50021 had also had a 'B' exam while it had been stopped out of traffic. After all the run-ups and a final check, all came good, and 50021 went back into service. – Job done!

Some weeks later I was informed that 50021 was stopped at Old Oak Common having suffered a total loss of coolant and was to be assigned to Laira for repair once again. When it arrived home a few days later we started the investigation into this failure. Almost immediately we found the sump was full of emulsified oil and coolant. We removed all the crankcase doors to find the fault, and the internal inspection began using torches. Unfortunately

the dockyard repair had failed. This was reported to management and the eventual decision from Head Quarters in Paddington, was that the loco would now go to Doncaster for a classified overhaul.

50021 returned to the Western Region on 22nd June 1978 fully overhauled and ready for its naming at Laira Depot on 31st July. This made it the 42nd fifty to be named.

Razor Blades to Razor Blades?

This recollection is about D410, 50010 'Monarch', released to traffic in 1967 and withdrawn at Laira depot at 09.00hrs on 27th September 1988. 'Monarch' never received Network SouthEast livery so was still in British Rail's large logo livery on its last duty, the 'Cornish Scot' (08.17 Penzance - Dundee Cross Country) service the on 30th July 1988.

On the day 50010 failed with low oil pressure near Bromsgrove. The power unit involved was IH6973 which had been rebuilt with a class 56 engine block and crankcase. This unique arrangement could have come about due to an error made at Doncaster Works, and may have played a part in the locos ultimate demise, as a fix would have required class 56 spares – not parts held as stock at Laira at that time. The recorded engine use was 6544 hours, about half that being expected from such a component. IH6973 was removed at Laira and sent away to Crewe Works for component recovery, allowing other locomotives to continue operating.

Its withdrawal caused a shortage within the class 50 pool of locomotives and power units in the repair pipeline. This in turn meant there were not enough locos available to meet Laira's commitments to keep the timetable running.

Following the removal of nameplates, 'Monarch' was just a nameless hulk. Over the next four years 50010 was stripped bare of all working component parts including its wheelsets – which were swapped for faulty sets from other locomotives. Ultimately this rendered the vehicle unsafe to be moved over the British Rail network to a scrapyard. So when the time came, it was decided to break 50010 on site at Laira, the only one of the class to be broken up here.

Coopers Metals of Salisbury won the contract to dispose of 'Monarch'. So in May 1992 the loco was moved from its location on the PAD Sidings against the stop blocks to a space where they could safely work. On day one, Coopers turned up with full bottles of acetylene and waste skips ready for the breaking work to be carried out, and within four days 50010 was just a memory. RIP 'Monarch'.

The Last Rites of Valiant and Thunderer

In the Autumn of 1991 it was announced that a class 50 railtour would run from Avon to Cornwall to celebrate the last running of Civil Engineers' DCWA pool locomotives; 50008 'Thunderer' and 50015 'Valiant'.

These 50s had not seen major works attention since their refurbishment at BREL Doncaster in the mid 1980s. Both were in reasonable condition having been regularly maintained at Laira, but both had high engine hours (over 10,000hrs in the case of 50015).

To add additional interest, both locomotives had been repainted in the January of 1991, 50015 receiving "Dutch" livery and 50008 a Laira variation on the standard BR Blue livery they had all been delivered with some twenty three or so years earlier. The pair had operated the Cornish Centurion (Jan 1991), Cornish Centurion 2 (May 1991), and The Hoover Hoop (October 1991) railtours during the year in their unique liveries.

October also saw the start of the "Leaves on the Line" season, and a class 50 hauling a single car (Ex DMU) over the South Devon and Cornish Banks, spraying "Sandite" on to the railhead to improve adhesion for following trains. 'Valiant' and 'Thunderer' did this on behalf of British Rail's Civil Engineering department, at times joined by any other high engine hours Network Southeast pool class 50s.

Once the leaf fall season was over it was clear that 50008 and 50015's careers were coming to a close with their last day in traffic defined as 23rd November 1991. Surprisingly Senior Management issued permission for both locomotives to have full repaints. This work was to use up paint already in Laira's stores left over from past work, the "Dutch" yellow and grey being left over from the Class 37 'G' exam programme in 1989. Nameplates were also painted black (with silver grey lettering) reflecting the standard applied to other locomotives owned by the DCWA Sector. The painting was by Roger Stevens from my "B" Shift.

Due to the lack of money and available paint stocks, the Laira Blue was a mix of various leftovers from the BR and NSE years. The recipe of colours produced something that was near to the BR blue shade but slightly lighter.

I was privileged to perform the last "A" Exams on 50008 and 50015 for their last day in British Rail service in preparation for The Valiant Thunderer railtour (Page 40). This outing was an overnight tour run by Pathfinder Tours. It started at 00.30 from Manchester, running to Newquay via Paignton with 47805. The 50s joined the tour at Bristol temple Meads at 04.19 hauling the train to the Dartmouth Steam Railway. However disaster struck when 50015's speedometer became faulty, during the run round at Paignton, usually a problem with the electronics or the axle mounted probe.

A delay then occurred whilst both fifties were swapped around so 50008 could lead out of the Devon seaside resort. Meanwhile 37142 in "Dutch"

DCWA's unique liveried 50015 'Valiant' and 50008 'Thunderer' lead the Hoover Hoop railtour past Little Haresfield on 19th October 1991. Photo: Ian Murray

livery was despatched from Exeter to head the train westward from Newton Abbott to Plymouth.
A call home ensured that the sight of a triple-headed railtour past my home town of Ivybridge was not missed by my boys.

Reaching Plymouth, the class 37 was released, and both fifties ran round to the rear. Sister 50033 'Glorious' in Network Southeast livery ran from Laira depot to head the train forwards to Newquay. The return leg departed the Cornish town at 14.20 with 50008 leading. On arrival at Plymouth, 50033 ran round the train and was placed inside 50008 and 50015 for the final run to Bristol Temple Meads arriving at 19.42. All three 50s then returned light engine to Plymouth Laira, where 'Valiant' and 'Thunderer's' adventures on British Rail came to an end.

The following day 50008 and 50015 were locked up, and stored while they were put up for sale on BR's disposal tender list.

At the time I was sure both would go for preservation, and yes as I write this in 2021 I am very pleased to report both were saved and are doing well! A great result.

End of the Line at Crewe

It was the summer of 1991 and I was on the early shift at Laira Plymouth depot . Many of the staff being on annual leave, my instruction of the day was to unload the last overhauled English Electric 16CSVT power unit from Crewe which had arrived overnight by road. I was given three off `B` shift staff and Des Spence our diesel 45ton crane driver to enable us to carry out the task. It was a bright summer morning which made a change for outside work. We all made contact with the lorry driver to give him the instructions of what we were about to do. Once we took the lift he was free to return up the M5 motorway towards home.

Des got the crane started whilst we made the old Retank wagon ready for use and checked the power unit lifting beam.

The heavyweight lorry and trailer were now backed into position so we could make ready for the removal of the large taupaline with the crane, once completed it revealed one IH6965 overhauled English Electric power unit this being the end of the line from BREL Crewe. The power unit was successfully lifted and placed onto the Retank wagon for shunting into number six road for unloading once again to the shop floor.

The shift was now over, an enjoyable day had been had by all out in the sunshine at Laira in glorious Devon.

Next day when on duty I was called to the technical Office who informed me that there was a problem with the new power unit IH6965, nobody had ordered it, nobody owned it, and nobody had paid BREL for the overhaul either.

Network South East was asked if they required it, the answer that came back was NO. The director of Procurement at Derby was therefore contacted and they put the power unit up for sale, meanwhile a notice was attached to IH6965 which said `under no circumstances removal of any components or materials be robbed from this unit`.

Some weeks later a call came through from the London North Western Railways at Crewe owned by Pete Waterman to ask of the details as they wished to make a bid.

The bid was successful but months and months went by before any further contact was made, so at Laira we therefore had to watch the timeline on the certificate of the class 50 lifting beam to ensure it

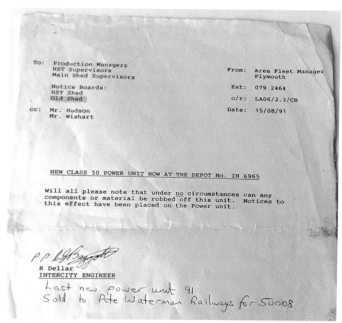

Confirmation from management that IH6965 must not be robbed or used. Photo: Val Woodhouse

was still in certificate for the final lift of the Pete Waterman power unit IH6965 to allow it to be dispatched north to the LNWR workshops at Crewe.

Once the power unit finally reached Crewe Heritage workshops, many months went by once again, but power unit IH6965 was finally put into Class 50 50008 `Thunderer` where it still is today.

Discovery During COVID 19

It is amazing when you do research how you can discover information that you never realised. Looking at the drawings of DP2 and the English Electric power unit IH5567 built May 1961 and fitted into that locomotive at the time of building, it had a Class 40 crankcase and crankshaft for a shaft driven cooling fan.

After the heavy collision at Thirsk, Yorkshire DP2 was then taken back to the Vulcan Works at Newton-le-Willows for dismantling. The power unit IH 5567 was however recovered and was rebuilt into the Class 50 engine pool having already seen some 360000 miles of service.

During the rebuild the crankcase was retained but the crankshaft (ex class 40) was exchanged for the production type fitted to all class fifties.

Power unit IH5567 saw service through the Class 50 fleet for the rest of its life having been fitted into the following fifties on the following years. 50017, 50050 -1970, 50049-1980, 50009-1982, 50016 --1985, 50029 -1990, then fitted into 50037 before it was written off `leg out of bed` and finally IH5567 was fitted into 50023 for the final journey to the scrap yard at Rotherham.

Blood Sweat and Fifties

D400 Comes to Plymouth

Anyone who has worked for British Rail over the last 26 years will have seen many changes in the locomotive fleet. Enginemen, engineers and management alike have had to adapt - particularly so if you were a Western Region man. This region of the BR system has always been different from the rest, not least its adoption of diesel-hydraulic traction, whereas the others went straight from steam to diesel-electric. Even today some claim the Western made the right choice.

Laira depot, at Plymouth in the heart of the Western region, has likewise seen many changes. It was one of the first diesel depots to be completed in the country, and it is also the only one to have been home to seven varieties of Type 4 locomotive, though not all at the same time. For the record these were Classes 41/42/43/46/47/50/52. The last to arrive was, of course, the Class 50.

Outside the old servicing shed (where the new HST depot has since been built) there was a short loco spur known as the sand road. It was normally used by visiting motive power or failures. A further use was to accommodate new types being used for train crew and workshop familiarisation. At this time the elimination of the hydraulics was in progress; the last 63XX out of Swindon, 6319, was already laid up. Replacement for the Type 2s, the Class 25 diesel-electric, was represented by 5179 in use for crew training purposes. 5827 soon followed, still in green with double white arrows.

It was 1973 when another stranger was due to come west, this time as a replacement for our Class 52 'Westerns'. Enter the English Electric Class 50, or D400's as they were in the original numbering. D400 first visited Laira in July 1973, on loan from Bristol Bath Road for both driver and engineer training. It reposed on the sand road and over the following months was swapped several times for 401 , minus its D prefix. After one such changeover 400 returned as 50050. D402 had been visiting Old Oak Common for the same reason.

Now, it takes time to adjust to change, and when we learned that the D400s were to replace our trusty 1000s we were not happy. Officially it was put across that the new type would be trouble-free and require less maintenance. Unofficially we heard the LMR would be glad to see the back of them, and this did not help in the adjustment. Our first impressions confirmed why they were not wanted in the north: the interiors were filthy, no place for crawling around in like monkeys whilst fault finding. The inertial filters were particularly bad, becoming blocked with carbon deposits. Another feature we did not like was that the door handles moved up to open the door, not pushed down as on other types, which is so much easier when your hands are full of tools and a hand lamp. This would not have been too bad but there were so many internal doors and the interior lighting was poor. '

To the electricians they were a nightmare. Although we did have a few diesel-electrics already, the 25s and 46s compared to a hydraulic which only had pump failure and earth faults to be dealt with, the 50s were something different. There was an electronic control system instead of the older style electro-mechanical or pneumatic, plus subsystems for slow speed control, current limiting and rheostatic braking. I remember spending a day on this braking system, the ultimate in braking, and only fitted to this diesel class. The main generators and traction motors also had to be understood. No-one at Laira had much knowledge of electronics on locos at the time, and so the CM&EEs representatives had to help out with repairs.

On the other band, the train crews certainly liked them on first impressions. To the drivers they were fast and powerful and also rode well. Unlike the Westerns, though, which had double bulkheads between driver and engines, they were noisier and less comfortable in the cabs, and the seats were set too low.

Our first allocation of a Class 50 at Laira was 50003 at the start of April 1974. At this stage many of the depot staff shied away from working on the new locos, preferring to stick to the familiar Westerns It was not surprising that the feeling towards the EE Type 4's was "give us a Class 52 any day". On arrival 50003 required a 'D' exam, which is quite an in-depth maintenance programme. This would really test our knowledge of how the loco worked! 03 was berthed on No. 6 road against the stop blocks - and seemed to stay there for ages, whilst several 52s were called in for the exam and returned back to traffic.

l began to wonder if the Fifty would ever turn a wheel again, the old joke for locos like this being to put grass cuttings under the wheels. But to be fair, all the staff had to start from scratch in getting to grips with these maintenance schedules, finding the right location on the loco, and then working out the best way of tackling the various jobs in practice. The management were in the dark, and the stores supply was nil - parts having to be requested from Crewe, Bath Road or Old Oak Common depots.

As more of the Class came to the Western more problems came to light, the dynamic braking system becoming an especial headache. But as always the Western found its own solutions, including the refurbishment programme of the early 1980's.

And with the timetable changes in May 1990, Laira became home to all of the remaining Class 50s.

Westerns Lose out to Hoovers

To many enthusiasts the year 1973/4 saw the beginning of the decline of the Western Region, as the withdrawal of the hugely popular Class 52 diesel-hydraulic began. Many of today's Fifty fans were weaned on bashing 'Westerns' overnight to the West Country.

The days of the 50 v 52 rivalry had begun; as had the takeover by the former of the latter's work, starting with passenger turns.

In February 1975 the WR decided to abandon steam heating and thus remove loco boilers. This left the 52s with just parcels, milk, stone and general freight diagrams. 1975 was also to be the last year for Westerns on summer Saturday holiday services, with the plan being for only thirty to remain in traffic by the year end. Tandem workings of both types could be seen that summer, and two examples on Newquay holiday trains I re-member were 1003 'Western Venturer' and 50043, and 50006 and 1056 'Western Sultan'.

During the early part of 1975 an industrial dispute at Bristol Bath Road over bonus payments for working on Class 50s saw many out of service. Thus although the 'Golden Hind' Plymouth to Paddington and return executives train was booked for a pair of 50s, in practice often only one was available. In consequence Class 52 substitutions could be found and on the 2nd of April 1005 'Western Venturer' worked both up and down trains.

At the same time all Paddington Class 1 commuter services were in Western hands, besides the clay and milk traffic.

Despite this minor revival, the overall trend was clearly in favour of the 'Hoovers'. As evidence for this, on 12th April 1975 50016 was transferred from Bath Road to Laira, causing the withdrawal of 1006 and 1050. But the 52s still had their moments. On 6th June a derailment at St. Austell blocking both lines meant that 1036, 1041 and 50028 were trapped in the far west and had to work a shuttle service to and from Penzance for a while.

A more typical memory is of 1041 'Western Prince' tackling Dainton bank on one engine, but despite a gallant effort stalling and having to be rescued by 50039.

1976 saw the arrival of HSTs for the Paddington to Bristol services, releasing 'Hoovers' for the West Country traffic. By the start of February 32 'Whizzos' remained, but from then onwards BR announced there would be no diagrammed work for the class. The writing was clearly on the wall. Two weeks later 1058 'Western Nobleman' was allocated on 1A09 Penzance to Paddington, consisting of steam heating stock, but the machine was removed at Plymouth in favour of E'TH-only 50047! Also about this time 50045 reached Laira from Crewe, but it lacked the ETH facility as its wiring was in such a poor condition.

There was a notable occurrence on 14th April 1976 when 1065 'Western Consort' plus 50009 worked the 1440 Plymouth to Paddington throughout. On 2nd June 50019 was derailed at Reading on the up 'Cornish Riviera Express', and the following day 1070 'Western Gauntlet' had custody of the train.

1010 'Western Campaigner' alongside the new order in the form of 50035 on Plymouth depot on 11th December 1976. By this time the transition was nearly over and the Wizzo would be withdrawn from service by the end of February 1977. Photo: Kevin Connolly

The summer is now upon us, and with a continuing high level of Fifty failures, there are not infrequent Class 52 substitutions. Not that the 'Westerns' had an easy ride. On a September night 1028 'Western Hussar' was booked on the 21 10 Penzance to Paddington sleeper; but at Truro it came to a complete and silent stand, and so an SOS was sent out. By chance, 50014 was stabled inside St Blazey's little old shed and so it was duly dispatched to the rescue. On nearing the stranded train the 50 was switched wrong-line in order to buffer up, but as it was dark and the sleeper had stopped on a severe curve, 50014 smacked into 1028. The rusting nose of 'Western Hussar' caved in, and the loco was withdrawn as the result, but 50014 was only superficially damaged.

At the start of 1976 eight Class 50s were still based on their native LMR by the mid summer all had migrated to the Western Region. There was now nothing much for the 52s to do. Six remained by the end of 1976, and the final day came on 26th February 1977, leaving the field clear for the Fifties to establish themselves and develop a following.

Headcode Matter

During the dissemination of the late 1950s British Railways Board ordered many types of locomotives from a variety of manufacturers; but they all had to be fitted with disc-type train indicators. These were white metal discs attached to each cab end and illuminated at night, in an arrangement of three across the top and one centrally below. They were hinged in the middle and so could be opened and closed, the resulting pattern identifying the type of train. This idea had been used by the SR and LMSR for many years.

However, soon after the pilot diesel locos entered service the BRB ruled in favour of a system that could identify train type, destination and number. This was the four character headcode featuring a panel built into the cab front, or, in the case of the Fifties, at roof level above the cab windows. The first character was a number showing the class of traffic, the second letter for the destinations, and the third and fourth numbers for the train number. This system lasted some sixteen years, but was dropped on 1st January 1976, mainly due to the introduction of the TOPS computer control, but also because of the disappearance of signal boxes and passing loops making identification en-route unnecessary. Depots throughout the BR system were told to fix the headcode panel to read 0000. However, on the Western the loco number was allowed to be shown in the panel instead. At Laira the Class 52s were all so treated, the only exception being 1023 'Western Fusilier'. On 18th November 1976 it was being made ready for a special from Kings Cross to York two days later, the 'Western Talisman' tour. The indicator blind was torn and so I obtained permission to fit the G39 'eyes' plastic strip with two white circles to permit backlighting. Later this was fitted as standard to all locos.

Many Fifties also carried their number, minus one zero, especially the ones allocated to Bath Road and Old Oak; but usually only for a short period before the G39 modification was carried out during the exam programme. 50030 was the last of the class to retain a working headcode panel. As an experiment

In the hazy sunshine of July 1975, the unrefurbished, and un-named, 50042 heads an up express at Reading with the headcode 1A30 displayed above the driver's cab windows. Photo: Tom Derrington

the headcode boxes on 50003 and 50035 were paneled over, with lamps mounted in the plating, So too was 50007, but at one end only, repair being needed due to accident damage.

During heavy repair (generally refurbishment) at Doncaster Works all headcode boxes were covered over, as many were leaking water through onto the driver's desk. Despite the fitting of the high-intensity headlight the two backlit 'eyes' were and still are retained.

Nameplates Ahoy!

During the summer of 1977 the Western region management made the decision to name all of the Class 50 fleet . In keeping with the tradition of naming locos with naval connections, the 50s were to be called 'Warships', as had the earlier diesel-hydraulic Classes 41/47/43. Many of the names had previously been carried by LMS steam 'Jubilees'. Although the appellation 'Warships' did not stick, the names themselves have helped greatly to boost the popularity of the Fifties.

Any enthusiast visiting Laira loco stores at Christmas 1977 would have had a treat indeed, in the form of seeing one hundred gleaming red and-silver cast nameplates, fresh from the presses at Swindon. At the time the names had not been assigned to individual locos, and it was my job to label each plate when the decision was made. We had the task of fitting plates not just to our own allocation, but also to the six based at Bristol Bath Road. A few naming ceremonies were planned, but in most cases the plates were fixed without fuss at the depot. First to escape from anonymity was 50035. An invitation had to be sent to the Navy for tile naming of '35 as 'Ark Royal' since it was anticipated that the famous aircraft carrier (based at Plymouth Devonport) would shortly be sailing on her last commission. The previous railbound owner of the name had been D601 - also based at Laira, and also one of the depot's favourites. During early January 1978 50035 came onto the depot for a complete external repaint, cabs included, plus the requisite 'C' exam. I was involved with all this. and with the management we tried to work out the measurements for fitting the plates from the drawings that Swindon had sent us - January 16th was the day that the first nameplate was actually attached. It was no easy task. The main problem was how to trace up the height and centre of the body. We measured other 50s but they were all slightly different. Eventually a template was made up square to the engine room roof bodyline. With a plate on each side any fitting that was not straight or square would be noticed at a glance. A further difficulty was the variation in plate length, from 'Indomitable' (50026) to 'Lion' (50027). In the end a centre tap hole was drilled, adjustments being

made with the one bolt before final fixing. A final touch was to remove the oval 'English Electric Leasing Company' plates, if the loco still carried them.

I must admit that seeing 50035 'Ark Royal' for the first time created a new impression on me: from now on it would have a character of its own. A further distinction was the fitting of white headcode panel lamps. The naming ceremony was then performed the next day by Captain Anson of HMS 'Ark Royal' at Plymouth North Road station. I believe that today's 'Ark' carries in its mushroom a nameplate from D601 arid a crest from 50035.

From then on I was involved with the naming of all but the last two of the class to be treated - but more about these later. In the meantime the other 98 plates lay gathering dust in a corner of the stores, as two full months elapsed before the next namings took place. This came about due to a request from RPPR Railtours for two 'namers' for their 'Derby Double' tour on 18th March. At the same time HMS 'Dauntless', the shore establishment near Reading, expressed an interest in a naming ceremony. This tied in well, since 50048, the loco booked for the name 'Dauntless', was due for an 'E' exam and full repaint.

50010 was also on the maintenance exam programme so this too would receive its name, 'Monarch'.

The pair duly emerged from Laira in the early hours of the 16th resplendent with their new names. Both headed east light engines to Old Oak, '48 later going to Reading for its naming ceremony. 50035 plus 50048 were booked for the doubleheader from Paddington to Derby. with 50010 as standby; but in the event 'Ark Royal' refused to operate in multiple with 'Dauntless' and so '48 and '10 worked the train.

From this date onwards I would take a note of each Class 50 coming on for repair at Laira and then go and ask the Chief Mechanical Engineer if he would agree to the nameplates being fitted. Of course, some locos were in Doncaster Works at this period, and the Bristol six (50039-044) were hard to remove from traffic. Sometimes it would only be one, sometimes two, but on 6th April no less than three 'Warships' were named: 50018 as 'Resolution', 50034 'Furious', and 50007 'Hercules' - a loco later to be surrounded by controversy over its name.

As it turned out, April 1978 saw the naming on no less than sixteen of the class: from then on it became a steady flow. Only after twenty had been done did we get our hands on the first of the Bath Road allocation, when on April 26th 50044 became 'Exeter'. May was also a busy month, the namings tally moving on to 33, the last being 50014 'Warspite' on the 30th. This name had last been carried by 'Jubilee' Class 4-6-0 number 45724.

By mid summer only a few were left unnamed. On August 4th the ex D400, 50050, became 'Fearless'; but at the last moment the Navy decided to have a naming ceremony, and so the plates were removed on the 7th and put back in the stores. Finally a suitable date for the ceremony was arranged, and on the afternoon of the 23rd 50050 was officially twinned with its naval namesake, the formalities taking place at the depot itself.

From then on the flow of namings became a trickle. No more were done in August, but on 1st September my own 50008 acquired the name 'Thunderer'. Six were left without names; of these, two were away at Doncaster Works, and two were Bath Road based.

These two were caught first; 50040 arriving for tyre turning on September 15th and becoming 'Leviathan', and 50042 receiving its 'Triumph' plates some three weeks later.

My final loco was 50029, which on 14th November emerged as 'Renown'. The other two were still on 'The Plant' at Doncaster, 50006 as the prototype for refurbishment, and 50011 undergoing classified repair. '11 was out-shopped in April 1979 with a new power unit, but without any treatment to the bodyside, which was very rough. It ran around in service until being made 'Centurion' on 20th August 1979. Meanwhile the 'Neptune' plates for '06 had transferred north to Donny on 20th June, but the exact date of fitting is not certain.

Whenever, it was the only Fifty to be named on the Eastern Region, finally entering traffic as 'Neptune' on 15th December 1979 - 49th to be named, but 50th and last to run in service (and also the only unrefurbished class member not to receive a name). Ironically these two locos were last to be named but first to be withdrawn.

Hercules III

This story concerns the third locomotive of the British Railways fleet to carry the name 'Hercules'. The first was the 4-6-0 steam loco 45703 of the London Midland Region; the second D822, a Western Region hydraulic built at Swindon in 1960. Just seven years later the frames were laid at Newton-le-Willows in Lancashire for the third 'Hercules'. D407 emerged anonymous, just another 100 mph D400 Class for use between Crewe and Scotland but today the loco has become the flagship of the Western fleet. To paraphrase a well-known saying: 'they seek him here, they seek him there, they seek 'Sir Edward Elgar' everywhere!'.

D407 was allocated from its native LMR to the WR at Laira in April 1974, one of the first to be transferred. Soon afterwards it was renumbered 50007. In 1974 it suffered serious damage to the cab at No. 1 end whilst shunting at Bristol. I can remember the managers talking to the welders and

sheet metalworkers to see if Laira could undertake the repair.

In the event two of my workmates proved that it could, '07 being berthed on No. 5 road stop blocks and the cab stripped out. Gradually the nose was brought back into shape.

One of our welders had worked in the RN dockyard at Devonport, and for him the work was easy when compared to patching up a ship.

At last the work was done, this being the biggest job ever achieved on Laira depot.

Even today the scars of the job can still be seen, notably on the buffer beam: but '07 still lives.

The name 'Hercules' was applied on 6th April 1978, the eleventh of the class to be named. Nearly five years later the loco emerged from the refurbishment programme in the new large-logo livery, 35th to be treated, but still just one of the crowd.

1984 changed all that. Early in the year it was announced that 50007 was to be renamed 'Sir Edward Elgar' and repainted in GWR Brunswick green, in connection with the 50th anniversary of the composer's death, and as a prelude to the Great Western 150th anniversary celebrations. Much controversy surrounded the move: some enthusiasts were out- raged, and the affair even reached the local newspapers. Whatever the rights and wrongs (for example the appropriateness of having 49 naval 50s and one musician), the decision stood.

The conversion process was swift, as the official naming ceremony was to take place at Paddington on 25th February. At 1600 hours on Wednesday 8th '07 lost its 'Hercules' nameplates, to be sold at Collector's Corner in Euston. By Saturday the loco had been given a suitable undercoat for its pre-war green livery, the top coat being applied the following day, the Sunday. On Monday the roof was painted black. as were the bogies on Tuesday, and the buffer beam in red on Wednesday. The lining out was completed on Thursday 16th with the next three days being occupied by bogie repairs and painting the inside of the cabs. The brass GWR-style numberplates were attached on the Friday and the nameplates on the following Monday. After inspection the new-look '07 left Laira for Old Oak at 0005 hours on Tuesday 21st.

Simon Rattle of the Birmingham Symphony Orchestra unveiled the 'Sir Edward Elgar' plaques on the appointed day, which was marred only by persistent traction motor problems. Since then '07 has become very well known, travelling the BR system to attend numerous Open Days. In 1985/6, for example, it visited Birkenhead, Canon Street, Carlisle, Coalville and Landore - to name but a few. In March 1987 an 'F' exam was carried out on 'Sir Edward', but the loco was not repainted.

Two years later sectorisation meant that 50007 had

to join the NSSA fleet in the Network SouthEast stable, which meant that a repaint into the standard livery was required. However, a decision came down from on high that a dispensation would be granted for '07 to retain its Brunswick green livery, as a special 'thank you' from Network SouthEast to the Laira staff for keeping the Fifties running: so it was that a full repaint was undertaken in time for the 21st anniversary of the BR Staff Association club at Laira. '07 was presented back to the NSE fleet, with all staff, past and present, attending the ceremony. All the Depot Engineers from the 1960s to the 1990s helped to plant a free of dedication. 50007 was well and truly Laira's flagship. As a footnote, the present fleet manager is an ex-Eastern Region man, and so '07 carries the embellishment 'Laira' on its buffer beams - after the Kings Cross 'top shed' tradition.

50040's Double Life

The first part of this tale dates back to 1981. After return to the WR following refurbishment at Doncaster Works each Fifty would be inspected on an audit, to see if the allocated repairs had been carried out to the satisfaction of the Region's CM&EE department. Usually there was no problem, but when 50040 'Leviathan' returned home shiny in its new large- logo livery in July 1981 the technical staff at Laira concluded that BREL's castings were not justified. The 'phone lines between Laira, Paddington (the WR headquarters) and Doncaster were red hot, until at last the Works accepted '40 for rectifications.

Coincidently, F&W Railtours were about to run their 'Doncaster Dart' tour from Plymouth to Doncaster Works, and it was partly at my suggestion that it would be a good idea to take '40 back to Donny via this train. Arrangements were made and accepted. Thus it was the gricers (AG among them) that were privileged to have superpower in the form of 50025 plus 50040 for the northwards leg of the tour, on 26th July. The 5,400 h.p. duo put in a splendid performance, appreciated by all. '40 was back on the WR within a fortnight, this time behaving satisfactorily. Sadly, both locos have now been withdrawn and cut up. The second part lakes place eight years on, in the twilight of 50040's life. In 1987 '40 was rechristened 'Centurion', because 50011, which had carried the plates, had been taken out of service for use as a power unit test bed at Crewe Works. This was an embarrassment to BR since a twinning ceremony with HMS 'Centurion' had taken place not long beforehand; and so the plates were transferred to 50040, the 'Leviathan' name no longer having a current naval association.

Anyway, on this particular day, 31st July 1989, I was out evaluating Eastfield-based 37188, on test following its 'G' overhaul at Laira. We ran light engine to Par in Cornwall, where on arrival our driver was asked by the signalman if we would go to Burngullow clay sidings. We all agreed and so he dropped the arm of the Par station starter and we powered away. At Burngullow the shunter said there were some clay slurry tankers to manoeuvre, and some defective ones to take back to St. Blazey depot.

This we duly did. It has always amazed mc that whatever the time of day and wherever you are there is always a rail enthusiast hanging around with a camera. Today was no exception, and as we approached Par once more I glimpsed a cameraman dashing from one side of the road overbridge to the other as we crawled up to the signal. From his figure l seemed to recognise him: truly, it was an old mate of mine from Lancashire. We exchanged tales by shouting in between shunting movements. 37188 was uncoupled and ran round the tanks before proceeding up the Newquay branch to back into the St Blazey Carriage and Wagon Yard.

On being released we ran back light to Par, where DCWA (Departmental sector) 50040 had just arrived on the Mondays-only 6M22 train, the 13.05 Truro to lnce & Elton fertilizer working. Was this the last stand in Cornwall for '40? Both locos stood side by side: the Class 37 spotless, the Class 50 looking very rough, its engine emitting blue smoke - a sure sign of heavy engine wear. I was about to suggest that we went on front to assist, but the lower quadrant starter dropped to give '40 the road. The 50 coughed out of Par with 6M22 leaving the station blanketed in smoke. I commented to the driver that we might have to give rear-end assistance to the train up Largin Bank; but when we were finally given the road there was no delay, and we passed '40 waiting in the through road at Plymouth station.

This was indeed the last stand for 50040 in Cornwall. Within three weeks the loco was taken out of service and never ran again. At the time of writing it lies cannibalised at Laira with sister 50010, waiting to be cut up.

Update: Those words were written in July 1990, and that was not the end of 50040's the story. The locomotive was initially moved to Booths scrapyard. But in 1992 it had moved to Coventry Airport where it was exhibited until 2008. After a change of ownership the former Leviathan was transported by road to Sims scrapyard in Halesowen where it was quickly cut up to provide parts for other preservation projects.

Dawn of a New Image

It is the 4th September 1980, and I'm on the early morning duty. The sun peeked over the roof line a fine summer's day lay ahead. In the foreman's office the buzz was that 50023 'Howe' had been delivered back from Doncaster after refurbishment - but sporting a bold new livery (unlike the first six to be treated). After receiving the day's work load most of us gathered outside on the oil road. A gleaming 'Howe' stood before us. resplendent in the 'new image' of wrap-round yellow cabs, grey roof, and large logo and number. Most pleasing to the eye; especially after the many years of the drab all-over blue livery (carried by all the 50s since new).

During the day most of the Laira staff, from CME to office workers, came out to admire the novel paint scheme As the sun rose further in the sky the loco shone, and many photographs were taken. Of course, many Eastern Region railways had already seen the new-look '23 on its test runs and on 1V93, the 0905 Edinburgh to Plymouth, booked for a Deltic to York where the Fifty would take over in order to return home to the WR and Laira. This duty was often used as a means of getting freshly-outshopped 50s back to their own territory.

For a while 50023 became Laira's flagship, just as D1023 'Western Fusilier' had been half a decade earlier. The Fifty celebrated its unique status by working the return leg of the RPPR 'Mayflower' railtour from Plymouth to Paddington later

in the month.

Within four years '23 was once more standard in appearance as all the Class had been repainted in the large logo livery. But, in 1986, 'Howe' again led the way when it was joint first to sport the Network South East colours (although it will probably return to Laira in the May 1990 timetable change), and carries the revised, darker blue NSE livery. Any further livery change is most unlikely; and so the only question that remains is will it, like its numbersake D1023, be the last in traffic and end up being preserved?

We shall have to wait and see.

Update: Those hopeful words were written in July 1990, but unfortunately while 50023 was initially bought for preservation, the project was abandoned and in 2004 it was cut up on site at the Barrow Hill Museum by the Harry Needle Railway Company.

Why 50149?

1986 witnessed the rise of Network East and its distinctive red-white-and-blue livery.

Most of the 50s were destined to end up in this garb, but some of the other newly-formed sectors were also responsible for a share of the work performed by the Class. With effect from the New

50025 'Invincible' and Large Logo 50040 'Leviathan' at Mexborough with F & W's 'Doncaster Dart' railtour on 26th July 1981. The trip bought enthusiasts from the West Country to Doncaster, and the Works open day. A combination of an unrefurbished and a refurbished class 50 as a pair on a train away from the Western Region was very unusual. .Photo: B Wynn for Pathfinder—Rail Photoprints

Year of 1987 "it was rumoured" Railfreight would take over responsibility for ten locos. They were to form a sub-class, 50/1, and be numbered 50101 to 50110 .

Arrangements were put in hand for the modification work to be done at BREL Doncaster Works. In the meantime no maintenance to the electric train heating equipment on the selected locos was to be allowed, and all operating expenses were to be charged to Railfreight.

The locomotives chosen were 50001/003/005/010/012/015/022/024/050, with the tenth still to be decided. However, it quickly became apparent that the gang of nine were not dedicated to freight work, but used just the same as the rest of the Class.

In April 1987 Railfreight sector confirmed it would put up the money to modify the first unit The selected loco would be one from the 'F' overhaul programme then underway at Laira, and all the work would be undertaken by the depot itself. In terms of modifications required, the 50/1 was to have regeared Class 37 wheelsets and traction motors, a derating adjustment to the power unit, and disconnections of the ETH apparatus.

So, which 50 would it be? 50050/028/044/049/043/005 was the provisional running order for the summer overhaul programme. As with all heavy maintenance to the 'Hoovers' I was actively involved, and played a part in each of the 23 'F' exams that Laira did. It was not until July that the regeared bogies were delivered, and what with staff shortages plus 50050 (just starting its exams requiring new bogies, it seemed that 'Fearless' would become 50101 - or would It be 50150? However, it was not to be. After some delay '50 was given ordinary bogies and entered the Network SouthEast fleet; and so the honour fell to the next in line, which happened to be 50049 'Defiance'.

Railfreight and the engineers from the Derby research HQ were pushing for a September release to traffic for trials, and so work began in earnest. '49 was birthed on No. 6 road stop blocks, and as well as the internal changes it was also to have the new Railfreight livery: Laira staff were to witness yet another new image. If the experiment was a success then this might be a lifeline for some class-members not down on the 'F' programme and thus facing early retirement.

In early September 50049 finally gave way to 50149, repainted in three-tone grey with the distinctive red-and-yellow chequer of the Railfreight General sub-sector. A first for Laira was having its own depot badge cast - of a ship, what else! By the required date of 20th September all the finishing touches were complete and '149 was handed over to the Derby engineers. The Class 50/1 made its first trial run light engine to Totnes and back in the early afternoon of the 22nd.

Its first real test came the next day on the afternoon shift. 47019, in charge of 6B43, the 1425 St. Blazey to Severn Tunnel Junction Speedlink freight, came light from Tavistock Junction Yard In order to collect 'Defiance' for testing. In the meantime the payload of the train had been made up to 960 tonnes. This proved almost too much for '149 and its debated 2,400 h.p. power unit on the 1 in 42 of Hemerdon bank, as it very nearly stalled; but worse was to come.

I was working on the next 'F' exam loco, 50043, when the call came through that '149 was off the road at Exeter. On being informed of the news I just could not believe it, but the foreman then came and told me and the rest of the breakdown gang to clear up what we were doing and make our way to the breakdown train. Our information was that 50149, 47019 and the leading wagon of the train had been derailed in Riverside Yard: a long shift was ahead. 50029 'Renown' was provided to power the breakdown train, and good progress was made to Exeter. We pulled up alongside the derailment and got out to examine the damage.

The two locos were going to be an easy lift as one bogie of each had just dropped off the road in a straight line. 'Defiance' was the first to be rerailed, and once this was achieved I climbed aboard to restart the engine. As we waited for the air brake pressure to build the bogie was examined and the decision taken to bring '149 home with us. '29 ran round and jumpered up to the 50/1, and then decoupled the breakdown unit.

Next came 47019, and as it was being rerailed the rest of 6B43 was shunted into an adjacent siding. By the time the loaded 75-tonne 'Tiger' clay wagon was back on the rails and our job complete it was the early hours of the next morning; at last we and the 50s could return to Laira.

The official Railfreight launch was not until 15th October, with adhesion trials planned the following weekend between Westbury and Warminster. Alas, disaster struck on the 8th, when '149 suffered a major engine failure at Yatton. 50014, working the Waterloo to Exeter route that day, was taken out of traffic to supply a replacement power unit (This being the last Fifty left with untreated mainframe fractures. 50006/011 had already been withdrawn). 'Warspite' was later scrapped as a result. By working round the clock '149 was restored to health in time, but the trials were not a great success. No more 50/1s were authorised and after eighteen months 'Defiance' was converted back to standard 50049 and returned to passenger work.

A Winter's Tale.

In the winter of 1981/82 many parts of Britain suffered blizzard conditions, from the north of Scotland right down to Cornwall. Heavy snow and

50049 'Defiance' was converted with regeared bogies to provide more torque (but a lower top speed) and trialed for freight use. Unfortunately the testing, which took place on the 18th October 1987, was not a success. On the day of the test Defiance with part of the test load passes Upton Scudamore. Photo: Nigel Hayman

ice everywhere caused British Rail services to be In chaos, but running wherever possible. The West Country was no exception. Laira was virtually besieged by all types of motive power and coaching stock suffering from a variety of freeze-up troubles. This story starts, however, further north and features 50030 'Repulse', still unrefurbished and in Rail Blue livery.

Whilst working a Paddington to Worcester service in whiteout conditions 50030 became a casualty with power earth faults due to snowy and generally damp conditions. Eventually it became stuck, and with a storm raging an SOS was sent for assistance. At the time '30 was only one of many locos similarly affected, from class 31s to HST power cars. After quite a while the train was rescued, but for poor old 'Repulse' it was only a beginning. Because of general chaos the loco was dumped in the open at Worcester and left to shiver over the weekend in sub-zero conditions.

It was decided to tow the stricken Fifty to Gloucester, but on arrival there neither they or Bath Road could provide attention as both had more than enough similar work to cope with already. So together with two class 47s, two Class 37s and a Class 31 it was dispatched home to Laira. On arrival '30 was berthed in No. 5 road to thaw out and have its faults diagnosed. It took two days before work

could be started, so bad was the freezing-up. The first check was on the cooler group. This showed all four radiator barks plus header tank needing to be replaced. After completing this work attention turned to the power unit, and here the diagnosis was failure of three turbochargers, two intercoolers, the water pump, many cylinder heads and all the water hoses and flexible couplings. Three weeks and many man hours later the weather was back to normal, but not so 50030; the work seemed to be endless! A final attempt was made to make the engine watertight. The engine and radiator were refilled and I turned the key to restart '30's power unit for the first time in a month: after all this time it was good to see light at the end of the tunnel. The engine was left to idle and became nicely warmed up, only for it to shut down without warning. A check on the radiator gauge showed it to be empty. A steady top up was made and the engine restarted; this time an Inch by inch survey of the engine block revealed a hairline fracture. After all that effort this was to be the end: nothing further could be done (this being in the days before Laira had the facilities to exchange power units) and so the loco was shipped off to Works for repair. Curiously although the refurbishment programme was well over half way complete, 50030 was not included at this juncture.

Hard Day's Night.

It is Friday the 31st August 1984; the time is 10.30 pm. For most people it is the end of the working week and the end of the day, but for those of us on the night shift at Laira the hard graft is just about to start. It is a clear but mild summer's night. Still, with a lingering reminder of the heat of the day. I book on for duty, and after changing into overalls I'm ready for work.

The Servicing Shed Foreman informs me that tonight I will be working mainly on Class 50s: seven are awaiting attention, together with one Class 45 and one Class 47. It should be borne in mind that there are two departments concerned with keeping locos running at a depot such as Laira, namely Traffic and Movements plus the CM&EE (Chief Mechanical and Electrical Engineer - in other words, repair and maintenance). Both must work hand in hand to achieve optimum results. After collecting my tools and lamps I make my way to No. 4 road in the main shed. The work will be carried out by a gang of two fitters, one electrician and a mate. 47053 is on the fuelling point topping up with only 26 gallons of fuel; while this is in progress I make a quick detour to survey the scene in the rest of the shed. There are seven Fifties out of service, these being:

- No. 1 road: 50032 (OC), on jacks for a double bogie change;
- No. 4 road: 50021 (OC), flashover repair to main generator;
- No. 5 road: 50014 (LA), ' B' exam;
- No. 6 road : 50012 (LA), 'B' exam; & 50017 (LA), repair to ETH generator;
- outside: 50015 (LA), await transfer to Doncaster Works;
- Cleaning shed: 50044 (LA), 'B' exam.

Now it's back to my night's work, which will consist mainly of footplate checks and the basic 'A' seven Fifties, most of which are already allocated to work trains the exam to next morning. These are:-

- 50048 (LA), 'A' exam, booked on Turn 213b: 05.38 Plymouth to Penzance (23.57 ex-Paddington), 11.05 Penzance to Paddington, etc.
- 50046 (LA), 'A' exam, booked on Turn 2111c: 07.07 Plymouth to Paignton empty stock, 09.45 Paignton to Paddington, etc.
- 50019 FP exam, booked on Turn 220b: 04.05 Laira to Exeter ECS, 0548 Exeter to Waterloo, etc.
- 50016 (LA), FP exam, booked on Turn 221b 05.40 Laira to Newborn Abbot staff train and local to Exeter, 0813 Exeter to Waterloo, etc
- 50025 (OC), FP exam, booked on Turn 205d: 06.08 Laira to Paignton empty stock, 08.55 Paignton to Paddington, etc.
- 50045 (LA), FP exam, spare: confined to local duties, awaiting transfer to Doncaster Works for classified repair.

- 50010 (LA), due t o arrive with loss of coolant problems.

These locos would clock up over a thousand miles between them whilst hauling the Summer Saturday holiday traffic, and it is our responsibility to see that they perform it without any mishap. It will be a busy night.

47053 has now come on to the pit for its inspection. 50048 draws up to take fuel, and as it has been out on the road for some time it takes on 745 gallons. The whole area is lit up by tower arc lamps making it just like daylight. 50046, 50016 and 50010 have already arrived, and, engines running, are waiting for their turn at the fuelling point. My mates I start on 50048's 'A' exam, and though not long back in service it looks a little grubby. I do the bogie examination first and note that all the brakes need adjustment. I then join my mate in the cab for a full brake test and engine run-up. Meanwhile 50046 has drawn up and proceeds to fill up with 270 gallons of diesel. I give the movements men the all-clear for 47053 and 50048, and as it is now midnight, we have a drink of tea while the two locos are moved out and replaced by '46.

On our return nothing has happened, the locos are in the same place as before. The reason is that the shunt crew on 08895 are busy drawing the chained-together old bogies out from under 50032 and depositing them in the next road, followed by collecting the replacements and reversing the procedure so that the loco can be reassembled. Outside 45012 is ready for the Plymouth to Penzance parcels, and a buffet car required at Penzance is being attached.

By now 'Ajax' is in place over the pit and we begin its 'A' exam. Again the brakes need adjustment and the windscreen wiper on the secondman's side is found to be broken and in need of replacement. We are working against time, and to add to the difficulty there appears to be confusion concerning 50010, which has drawn up to take fuel : obviously the Movements side are not aware of its loss of coolant problem. In any event, 50021 is already berthed in No. 4 road, and has been there for a week with its flashover damage, meaning that space is at a premium. Therefore it is decided to concentrate on locos with booked workings later on in the day.

50025 maneuvers up to the fuelling point, and we examine the brakes while they are on: once more adjustment is needed.

In the interim 'Invincible' has taken on 260 gallons of fuel. There is still no sign of 50019 arriving back at Laira after its day's labour yet according to the plan it should be the first to be booked off again in the morning .

As we complete the checks on '25 I notice that '32 is being lowered onto its new bogies and across the

Laira depot has raised platforms with working space underneath allow servicing work to be undertaken readily on all parts of a locomotive. In this case 50050 is just about to begin its transformation to D400, sponsored by Rail Magazine. Photo: Carl Looker

other side of the shed the overhead crane is lifting the replacement ETH generator into 50017.

It is now 2.30 am and we take our meal break. 50016/019/045 remains to be serviced, along with 50010 if we can find time. During our absence '25 plus '46 are shunted out and '16 plus '45 shunted in. 'Barham' takes 577 gallons of fuel and 'Achilles' 299 gallons.

Looking over the former it is found that very little attention is needed. whereas the latter needs its brakes adjusting.

This done I tell my mate that I will go and have a look at 50010 whilst the next shunt is completed. It had arrived after piloting 50035 on the up sleeper (2135 Penzance to Paddington). I check the coolant level first and find this to be satisfactory, and so check the radiator and engine for leaks; again nothing amiss. Next I examine the radiator fan speed, as perhaps the coolant had boiled away. Once more this was not the problem, and so I return to No. 4 road where 50019 is just arriving. As stated earlier, 'Ramillies' is booked off at 04.05, but, surprise surprise the brakes need adjusting. I decide I had better report to the foreman about both 50010 and 50019, as it might well prove preferable for the latter to swap duties with another 50 already available.

Unfortunately this will not be possible as Movements have committed 50019 to train 5O02, the empty coaching stock for the first up Waterloo

service. Time is not on our side and the eyes are getting a little heavy. The engine needs 25 gallons of oil, and by now the Exeter crew are standing by and have to wait for us to finish the exam.

Our foreman returns to tell us that 50010 will come in on No. 4 pit behind 50021; we will have a second look for coolant leaks. The final shunt is made and '19 leaves the shed trailing smoke, clouding the light of the shed lamps. 'Monarch' arrives, and a glance at the bogies reveals the need for a complete reblocking of the brakes. Again this is relayed to the foreman, who says that 50010 will be stopped for further investigation.

It is now the time to write up the logs and worksheets. The TOPS computer shows that Laira's 50027 is stopped at Tyseley for derailment damage, whilst 50029 also one of ours - is on Old Oak Common for a main generator change.

It is now 5am and time for a wash before booking off and going home to bed. 'Good morning, Fifty followers, I hope you all enjoy your summer Saturday travels Perhaps next time you will spare a thought for those nightshift men who prepared your locos for traffic.

By way of a postscript I was picking blackberries with my family at Totnes that afternoon when the unprecedented sight of 58002 hauling a failed HST on the 12.10 Liverpool to Penzance rattled past on the nearby line. I immediately hurried back to Laira.

Men of the Greyhounds

This is a tale of the 'Green Badge' men.

Many of our older Class 50 drivers are proud of their 'roots' on either the Western or Southern Regions. With the rise of the Sectors the old Regions have taken a back seat, but on the ground the old rivalries still exist. Both Exeter and Plymouth had SR and WR depots, deriving of course from the Great Western and London & South Western Railways.

In both cases it is the WR bases that have survived, men from Exmouth Junction now working at Exeter St. Davids, and Plymouth Friary men now at Plymouth Laira. This does not deter the SR crews from flaunting their heritage as successors to the 'Green Badge' elite, who drove Bullied 'Merchant Navy' and 'West Country' Classes on the 'Atlantic Coast Express'; and, in earlier days, the Drummond 'Greyhounds'. Today the SR men have a reputation for driving rather differently from their WR colleagues: on the Waterloo route this is termed 'hard and fast'.

One Sunday morning in the summer of 1988 I had a cab ride on the 09.40 Exeter to Waterloo, care of a 'Green Badge' driver and 50021 'Rodney' (based at Old Oak at the time). Our train gets the right of way and with a blast on the horn we accelerate out of St. Davids and up the steep 1 in 37 bank to Exeter Central (the erstwhile Queen Street, the SR station). The driver thrashes '21 very hard, roaring off between the thirteen station stops en-route. At Salisbury there used to be a crew change, but now Exeter men go through to Waterloo and back. From here the road is fast and straight, and 'Rodney' is clearly working well with the load of eight Mark 2s. As we meet the line from Bournemouth at Worting Junction on the edge of Basingstoke, we find we are running alongside one of the modern generation Class 442 'Wessex Electrics'. This is the first time l had seen one of these sleek new EMUs. The driver comments that we will give the unit a run for its money into Waterloo.

Honours are even under yellow signals into Basingstoke station, but we are first away from the stop. '21 is given full power to lift its train towards the 100 MPH line speed limit, as the road ahead is green. I slide the co-drivers window down to have a look back, and see that the 442 is gaining on us. despite its quicker acceleration we have the measure of it, springing like a Greyhound towards Woking. the final stop before the stop-go crawl into Waterloo. Even so. the EMU just manages to draw ahead. the drivers acknowledging each other. After Woking both trains are running between sections as the track gangs were busy tidying the permanent way in preparation for the heavy Monday morning traffic. It seemed like we had lost the race. but then at Vauxhall the EMU was passed at a stand, waiting for access to its platform at the terminus. We pull up to the buffers on time. A well earned tea break meant that our crew were refreshed to return on the 14.10 down service, with Old Oak's 50036 'Victorious'. Whilst preparing for the homeward journey it was found that the loco needed coolant, and '36 had to be topped up again at Salisbury and back on St. Davids stabling point. But the 50 had accomplished its task on time, a tribute to the doughty 'Green Badge' men and their 1980's Greyhounds.

Waterloo Sunset

Update: At the point when this story was penned there was still some uncertainty about BR's plans for the class 50 and the traction requirements for the Waterloo — Exeter route in light of the Government's funding settlement for the organisation.

As it is now certain that the Exeter to Waterloo line will be the last bastion of Class 50 activity, let's focus now on the route and changes of diesel motive power.

It is interesting to note that the first diesels to take the LSWR way to the South West were, like the 50s, the products of English Electric. Built in between 1950 and 1954 for the Southern Region. 10201, 10202 and 10203 pounded the rails out of Waterloo for a while, but when full dissemination came in the 1960s it was the Maybach-engined Class 42 diesel-hydraulics that were given control of the SR services to Exeter and beyond. These Warships, some in maroon livery, some in green, and by bearing names today held by the 50s, would haul mostly Bulleid and Maunsell green-liveried stock. steam heated and vacuum braked. Newton Abbot shed (code 83A) was the base for much of this operation.

The most famous train on the route, 'The Atlantic Coast Express', last ran one September Saturday in 1964. This year also marked the downgrading of the line, surely a mistake with stations closed and sections of line singled. In the early 1970s Newton Abbot shed closed, the work being transferred to Laira (84A, as was), and the Class 42: were phased out.

In their place came SR Class 33s based at Stewarts Lane, Hither Green and Eastleigh.

The coaching stock also changed, dual braked and dual heated Mark 2s in blue-and-grey livery. This was definitely an improvement for the traveler, but the Waterloo to Exeter line remained a secondary route.

A revival of fortunes has taken place in the 1980s, starting with the introduction of Fifty-power, reducing the schedulers to the fastest since the days of the limited-stop 'ACE'.

Crew training with the 50s began in 1979, involving

men from Exeter, Salisbury and Eastleigh. Old Oak loaned a loco to Stewarts Lane for familiarisation at that end of the line, 50004 being the first to venture south of the Thames. Many drivers did not get on well with the Class at first, sending the locos back to the WR for attention to even the slightest defect - much to the consternation of the operating authorities.

Now the 50s have held away for a decade, allowing themselves to be master of this demanding route. With them have come other improvements, such as the reopening of stations (e.g. Pinhoe and Templecombe) and the reinstatement of passing loops (e.g. Tisbury). Affairs must have been improving as one day in April 1981 50014 worked the 0910 Waterloo to Exeter service complete with an 'ACE' headboard. But it was 1986 and the arrival of Network Southeast that has had the biggest impact - and not just in terms of being a lifeline for the Fifties. Today the route in the most prosperous it has been for many years, and with the Channel Tunnel traffic is expected to rise dramatically.

A £55 million upgrading has just been sanctioned, and so from 1992 a new form of motive power and coaching stock will be needed. 'Fearless', 'Dreadnought' and the rest have done their job well, but time is now running out for them; their Waterloo sunset is at hand.

Ups and Downs, Western Style

It was the October school half term in the West Country, and as usual it was raining. On a Wednesday just before I had some leave due, I was instructed to ride 50002 'Superb' to Paignton, to check on its persistent low coolant problems. Having booked on and assembled tools and snack, I made my way to outside on No. 1 road at Laira. There was '02, sheltering under the bogie hoist, and in the company of 45144, 47 151 and 50016. Our train was 5A48 08.10 off shed, 08.40 off Laira Carriage Sidings empty stock to Paignton, to form 1A48 - the 11.05 Paignton to Paddington 'Torbay Express'.

After checking the coolant level I started up 02's engine and then had a look at the CU4 unit to make sure the radiator fan speed and radiator shutters were all functioning properly.

The driver arrives, this being a single-manned turn, and after he has performed his checks we set off for the carriage sidings, the windscreen wipers flicking to and fro.

At the dummy signal 45144 is waiting to enter No. 1 sidings we also wait and then enter No. 4 road. Our train comprises eight assorted Mark 2s. Whilst we couple on and perform the brake test the Class 45 does the same over on its air conditioned stock, which will form the 11.05 Plymouth to Newcastle. The ETH button is depressed to warm the train en-route and then revs up 'Superb's' engine before applying power and threading out of the sidings. Using 1,000 amps we cross the down main line, and on an old wreck in the adjacent River Plym estuary ('The Laira') where I notice that shags and cormorants are nesting.

The AWS bell rings clear and we head off for Hemerdon. I make a quick check in the engine room to see if there are any faults, but everything seems fine. Back in the cab speed is down to 32 mph on the steepest part of the bank. but the amps are rather high at 2,200.

However, despite the wet rails and blowing leaves there is no slipping. On the night of its fateful run in 1983, 50041 nearly stalled here on icy rails; it if had, might it have avoided the spectacular derailment at Paddington?

As built, the Class 50s had tractive effort control so that drivers could regulate power more precisely to prevent slipping and thus drive with more confidence. But this system was unreliable and was removed during the refurbishment programme.

The AWS again rings clear, this time signifying that we are approaching the summit loops. 50002

Mike and Dicky Daw at Waterloo with 50050 (as D400) about to head west with the Atlantic Coast Express. Photo: Mike Woodhouse Collection

is running well, and we canter down Rattery bank and take the through road at Totnes, where we pass 50009 'Conqueror' on the 0635 Bristol to Plymouth. Coasting through the station power is applied for the assault on Dainton, but the AWS goes for a 20 mph track slow. I take another good look around the engine room and find a small coolant leak, but it is not severe enough to warrant the loco being taken off its duty. As we slog up the incline 31264 rolls downhill with a special freight for the Royal Naval Dockyard: later in the day the interloper ventured even further west, being put on a Railfreight turn to St. Blazey. Back at Dainton we enter the tunnel at 42 mph and on 2.000 amps. Down the other side we go, dropping past Stoneycombe Quarry (which is quiet today) and on towards Aller Junction. This is well and truly lower quadrant country, but not for much longer: the year is 1985, and this is the start of the last remaining pocket of semaphore signals on the Great Way West to Plymouth. At Newton Abbot West Box we draw to a stand before the signal clanks off to allow us onto the down relief road. 'Superb' runs round, couples up, and we receive the right away for the Paignton branch. Snaking over the 10 mph crossovers I tell the driver that I will ring Laira on arrival to inform control that the loco is able to continue its diagram on the 'Torbay Express' to London. The driver and guard are booked through to Taunton.

The train ambles along the branch in the heavy drizzle towards the seaside - not that the beaches will be crowded today. I am dropped off at Paignton platform, while '02 continues to Goodrington Sidings in order to run round. 50020 'Revenge' is waiting in the up platform with the 1010 to Plymouth. I make my tea and report to Laira, also telling them that '20 is on my return train. 'Revenge' being restricted to local working for observation at this time.

Once again I join the driver in the cab of a Fifty. At 10.05 the engine is started, disturbing the seagulls. The crossing gates go down, the horn is sounded. and we make a spirited start out of the resort. Climbing the bank out of Paignton the amber wheelslip light comes on, and with speed at 45 mph power is eased. Stone bridges pass by as the curving tracks wind their way towards Torquay. Although colour light signals are in evidence the semaphores remain in use in the final few months of their lives. Few passengers await our train at Torquay, where on the other line 31417 runs in on an Exeter to Paignton local. '20 gets on the move again, but the AWS alarm sounds for a stretch of new track: the driver is not quick enough cancelling it and so the brakes go on, speed dropping to 20 mph. Passing Aller Junction we run side by side with 50036 'Victorious' on the 0730 Penzance to

Aberdeen. '36 will take No. 4 road under the wall, as it is non stop (this area has now been tarmaced over to make a car park). We are cautioned under amber signals into Platform 3.

Before 50020 runs round I notice the lampman refilling the oil supply for the signal Iarnp wicks. We wait for a while to connect with the 08.45 Paddington to Penzance HST.

Today the service is headed by power car 43002 'Top of the Pops', and the set includes executive saloon 40513 used for transporting VIPs. We follow the HST out to Aller Junction, and, when the signal clears, 'Revenge' is opened up to tackle the climb to Dainton Tunnel.

Autumn leaves blow around to show that the weather is drying up. With the summit in sight the track ahead from the driver's window looks like a great hump through the tunnel bore. We can see that the signal on the far side is on, and the repeater on the tunnel mouth sounds as we plunge into the gloom. With the brake on the train slows to a crawl, which continues all the way into Totnes. The HST does not stop there but we do, and so afterwards the route is clear. Rattery is the last main climb of my journey, and I talk to the driver about the old days and trackmen. At one time trackmen on the up line at Marley Tunnel (twin bore and of cosmetic use only, located near the summit at Wrangaton) would drive a wooden stick into the ground near the tunnel mouth and attach an old rag to it, which would flap as a train approached and thus warn them to stand clear.

Inside the tunnel the pinpoint of light grows steadily larger, and the driver tells me to watch the trailside as we leave the tunnel. With the train pushing the air out of the single bore at a great rate the trees and shrubs are blown violently as we emerge.

Another twenty minutes and we pull in to Plymouth, on time. '20 now has to remove the first three coaches and attach them to rear of the 09.32 Penzance to Paddington 'jumbo' as it arrives. In readiness we run out to Plymouth west end and wait; it is not long before the jumbo hoves into view in the care of 50033 'Glorious'. The job completed we return to Laira shed: the South Devon banks have been tamed for another day.

Day Return to Penzance

It was a warm summer's afternoon, the date sometime in 1975 or 1976. After bookings on at Laira at 14.30 I was told I was to take the stopper to Penzance. in order to monitor 50002, which was suffering from engine stopping faults. The loco had just been transferred from Old Oak Common, and typically for the machines not long off the LMR, it was in a rather grubby condition. Of course, at the time '02 was unnamed and unrefurbished. After obtaining tools and tea can I made my way to No. 6 road where the loco stood outside the shed, ready for its booked turn, 2C74 the 16.45 off Plymouth. The cab interiors were in a poor state, dirty and showing some corrosion to the desk fittings, possibly indicating that the loco had lain out of use for a long time. The reason became obvious when I entered the engine room, as a new main generator had recently been fitted at Crewe Works. Before setting off I checked the levels of coolant, engine sump oil and engine governor oil. The four character headcode was still operational, and when I confirmed the train reporting number with the crew this was rolled up to order. The engine was started and final checks made. There was time in hand, and so the driver suggested we move off shed early and make a cup of tea at North Road station.

The 16.45 was actually made up of five coaches, and was primarily used by school children and shoppers from East Cornwall. It called at all stations, including the Halts at Dockyard, Devonport, Keyham and St. Budeaux, and then all points west. The guard's whistle blows and we pull out on time. 50002 ambles along past the Naval dockyard, where I notice a large collection of surface ships and submarines, all with names but as yet no association with the Fifties. On towards the Royal Albert Bridge spanning the River Tamar; a brake application, is made to bring our speed down to the required 5 mph. Half way across and we are in Cornwall.

There is no sign of any faults yet, but I don my earmuffs and disappear into the engine room to observe as power is applied after the Saltash stop. Oil pressure remains steady at 60 psi. The heat thrown out from the engine is breathtaking, with the exhaust pipes glowing cherry red: one set of pipes is white hot, indicating the engine timing is out, a point to be booked. All the turbochargers are working together at 9 psi. As yet there is nothing to indicate the cause of the shutdown problem, and so I go out past the dirty inertia air filters and take in the fresh, cool air.

We continue our journey westwards, running into the setting sun, which suggests it will be a fine day tomorrow. Arrival at the Penzance terminus is scheduled for about 7pm, and we approach the station a few minutes down. I resolve to inform Laira of the position on arrival, as the next leg of '02's diagram is 1A01, the 21.35 up sleeper throughout to Paddington. We are greeted by the station supervisor who says we are to take 50035 back with us in multiple as far as Plymouth, as it is suffering a low power fault which will need to be rectified at Laira. It is agreed that we will run round to the flower bay under the sea wall and collect '35 and then couple on to 1A01 before having our tea

break. The Penzance Class 08 pilot shunts the train, and then the pair of Fifties (connected in multiple) back on and their engines are shut down. Now it's time for tea.

I decide to go around both locos and check all oil and coolant levels prior to departure.

By now the sun has sunk into the Atlantic, and the passengers are on board for their nocturnal journey to the Metropolis. We ease out of the station gently with theoretically 5,400 bhp and a trailing load of twelve for 470 tons. 50002's engine shuts down; we restart and I go into the engine room. The engine stops again. A second restart is made and we struggle into St. Erth. I inform the driver that it appears to be an electrical fault now that we are working in multiple. We therefore decide to uncouple the multiple jumper cables, using '35 to provide the ETH only and '02 for traction. '02 picks up its train with a struggle, now pulling an extra 117 tons as well as the heavy train. Fortunately there is no more trouble from 50002, and so there must be a jumper fault on one of the locos.

The problem now is that we are losing time. As our secondman is a passed Class 50 driver the decision is taken to use '35 for tractive power but driven from its own cab; in other words working the Fifties in tandem, not in multiple. Now it is right away to Plymouth with no further mishaps, '02 working well and '35 limping on its low power. At last Devon is reached, and as we pass Saltash we have a clear view of the Royal Albert Bridge all lit up. The night is clear and starlit. and this gives reflections in the water at the dockyard.

On the final approach to Plymouth the signal is against us arid we stop, before the yellow aspect shines and the route indicator displays Platform 7. We are fifteen minutes down.

Our duo are detached whilst 50004 waits patiently in Platform 8 to take 1A01 forward. We slip out of the lights of North Road station and I get ready to see our duty foreman and then sign off.

Mishaps with the Milk

Trains of milk from the West Country to London ceased in 1980: the sight and sound of the distinctive six-wheels tankers squealing round the sharp curves in Cornwall is very much a thing of the past. Now the traffic goes by road. Some would call it progress.

Three incidents with milk trains come to mind, separated by over fifteen years. Firstly we go back to 1963 and the severe winter of that year. It was sometime in March and I was nearing the end of my turn on the early shift at Old Oak Common when a call for help came in from the Unigate Dairy at Wood Lane in White City. The trouble turned out to be a pair of Class 43 'Warships'. D818 'Glory' and D862 'Viking', which were booked on the 1440 empty tanks to the St. Erth creamery but were unable to reverse into the sidings. In fact both were assigned for repair and were travelling home to Laira for attention.

My route home out of London passed close by, and so I was asked to fix the recalcitrant hydraulics and then travel forward on them to Greenwood. It did not take long to diagnose the fault, and the milk train was able to set off only thirty minutes late. Many years later, after the hydraulic 'Warships' had all been scrapped and I had been reallocated to Laira, two breakdowns on the milk took place. On this particular Sunday afternoon a cool wind was blowing. Our depot was very quiet: not a hammer or spanner could be heard. l was one of only two fitters assigned to this shift. Examples of Classes 46, 47 and 50 were stabled, dormant, all around. At about 6.30pm the phone rang with the news that 50036 on the Kensington milk had become derailed at Totnes while backing into the siding to collect further full tankers. That was the end of the peace and tranquility, and the depot was transformed into a hive of activity. The 'on-call' breakdown foreman arrived, as did the night retailing gang. It was the early hours of the following morning before they all returned, bringing 50036 in for repair (the break-down train loco having been used to take the milk forward). When the Fifties arrived from the LMR the St. Erth to Kensington milk service became the preserve of the Class 52 'Westerns', since no heating was required. After their demise the ETH-fitted 50s were frequently used, along with the more

appropriate 47/0s. On this particular day 50017 was allocated to the tip service, whilst I had the job of accompanying un-named 50013 plus 50042 on the 10.23 stopper from Plymouth to Penzance, both locos being on the test. During the Truro stop the station supervisor came up to us and said that '17 had refused to start and needed rescuing. Arrangements were made for '42 to be detached at St Erth to take charge of the 1610 service to Kensington. with '13 continuing alone for the last few miles to Penzance.

The milk train crew were waiting for us as we run up to the signal box at St. Erth. 50042 is quickly unhitched and makes its way to the milk siding and the stricken 50017. I decide to travel back on the milk, and when the train is ready I stop for a tea break. Sitting on a bench on the station platform in the sunshine I watch as 50013 rumbles in with an up passenger. Our driver informs me that we will follow '13 up the line, stopping off at Lostwithiel to pick up more tankers. This we duly do, and while the dead Fifty is transferred to Laira and I sign off, the milk rumbles on in to the night in order that Londoners can have something to put on their cornflakes.

Today we have been booked on a planned recovery operation, following the derailment the previous day of part of a Meldon Quarry stone train at Bow, on what was left of the 'Withered Arm' network of LSWR lines. The wind was blowing hard, it was decidedly cold, and there was sleet and rain to contend with too. Snow and freezing temperatures had been forecast for later on. We were all kitted up

An unrefurbished 50026 prepares to shunt the Milk Tanks that form the 16.42 St. Erth - Clapham milk train at Lostwithiel on 26th June 1979. Photo: Rail Photoprints

with hats, overalls, boots and thick winter coats - it felt like we were off for a day in a labour camp. There was no sign of the train, and so a suggestion was made the one of us ring Laira to find out if it had set off yet. On doing so the reply was that it was just about to leave, as they were awaiting the arrival of one member of the gang who lived in Cornwall. It be another 20 minutes before it reached lvybridge.

A Busman's Day Out

It may seers rather odd that a railwayman should choose to spend his day off travelling the metals, but this particular journey was a rather special one. The famous Settle and Carlisle line was under threat of closure, and a special being run from Plymouth seemed an ideal opportunity to ride this magnificent route before it was lost for ever.
So it was that a group of friends and l boarded the F&W 'Scenic Settler' railtour shortly before the 4am departure one cold and frosty morning in April 1984. The open-plan Mark 1 coaches had windows running with condensation, but this at least promised that we would to warm for the day ahead. Just before the head count we nipped to the front of our train to see what motive power had been provided by Laira. Why, it was my favourite, 50008 'Thunderer'; how thoughtful! Under frosted sleepers our 1Z49 special slips out of Plymouth. The journey north and east is uneventful, and mostly a chance to catch up on the lost sleep. Beyond Bristol, through the talk was of the Lickey Incline, which today had a speed restriction at the start of the climb: perhaps the assistance of the bankers - usually a pair of Class 37s - would be called for. It seemed so, for the train slowed on the approach to Bromsgrove, at the foot of the bank; but then the train crew realised that no bankers were on duty this Saturday, and so the Fifty would have to haul the heavy load on its own.
'Thunderer' lived up to its name as it took full power for the ascent, and made a spirited attack on the stiff gradient. Even so, speed gradually fell to walking pace, and we all began to wonder if '08 would stall. At last the special clawed its way over the summit at Blackwell, the loco having given its all. We gave a cheer: the Laira Fifty was in good fettle as, of course is only to be expected! '08 was now in its native region, the LMR, and soon we arrived under the wires at Birmingham New Street. From there 1Z49 made its way to Bescot Yard, and as we gently ran through we catch sight of the virtually brand-new 56113 and 58010. We then rejoin the WCML and '08 treated us to a fast sprint to Crewe. from where it is to be relieved by a Class 47. Crewe had been D408's base from new, and this was the second time it had been back since its transfer to Laira a decade previously. The other

occasion had also been on a railtour from Plymouth, when in November 1979 the unrefurbished and freshly repainted 'Hoover' took a trainload of railfans to the Works Open Day. As '08 retired to the depot to join the other varied products of English Electric's Vulcan Foundry (not far up the line, at Newton-le-Willows). 47537 'County of Gwynedd' backed onto our train. Appropriately enough the Brush was allocated to Crewe Diesel depot. As it got stuck in to the journey north, we are told that we are to travel the S & C from north to south, since two other specials were to use the route in the opposite direction. Carlisle is reached some twenty minutes late, but there was still time for a lunch stop.
Then we were away again, and quickly onto the S & C metals at Potteril Bridge Junction.
The weather was most uninviting: bitterly cold with frequent sleet showers, yet still with the odd snatch of sunshine. As we approach Lazonby the first of the northbound specials is passed, hauled by EE stalwarts 40009 and 40033. Despite the weather the scenery is breathtaking, with Cross Fell, lngleborough and Perlyghent capped in snow. As we breast the summit of the long climb at Ais Gill the talk is of the other excursion, which is reported to be steam-hauled, by either LNER A4 'Sir Nigel Gresley' or SR West Country 'City of Wells'. We catch a glimpse of the old turntable at Garsdale, complete with fencing to stop locos being spun around in the gales. In the event it was the latter that filled our open coach windows with steam as we slowed for a photographic stop at Dent. The signal box there now looked decidedly derelict, but there is no time to investigate as the stewards soon shepherd us back on board. At Blea Moor two Class 31s 31152/209, are stabled but with engines running. Then we cross the majestic Ribblehead viaduct: would this be for the last time? Heading down into the foothills we take the freight-only branch from Hellifield to Blackburn, and pass by the Clitheroe cement terminal where the last surviving Clayton Type 1 is still employed as a shunter; but it was not on view today.
By now 50008 must be getting ready to leave light engine for Stockport, where it will take charge of 1Z49 once more. We thread our way through Blackburn and Manchester Victoria, and catch sight of more Class 40s at Miles Platting before taking another freight branch, the Aston Moss North Junction spur into Stockport. 'Thunderer' was there waiting. and after the usual photographing the Laira loco heads tor home. For me this 18-hour railtour to the S & C was a most enjoyable 'busman's day out'.
Since then, Class 50s have themselves traversed the line on excursions: and happy to relate, the route has now been reprieved and can enjoy a bright and

secure future, Maybe one day our preserved 50 will delight the railways as it pounds up the 'Long Drag' and through the desolate moors, just as 'City of Wells' did on our day out?

Update: The Clayton is now preserved at the Severn Valley Railway and regularly operates alongside their extensive fleet of class 50s… And several 50s have returned to successfully tackle the Long Drag in preservation.

The Road to the Scilly Isles

Even though there are no railways on the Scilly Isles, perhaps 50014 'Warspite' was attempting to get there one hot day in July 1984 when it derailed itself in the Scilly Isles flower bay at Penzance. Even being named after a nuclear submarine did not seem to have helped. Instead, a call was made to Laira for the breakdown unit to attend.

As part of the team I was detailed to help with the rerailing of the stricken 'Warspite'.

47334 was provided for the breakdown train, and we made steady progress westwards, arriving at the Cornwall terminus at 10 am. The temperature was already an the 80s. Firstly we walked over to the loco to estimate the damage and how long it would lake to put the ll7-ton beast back on the rails. No. 1 bogie, at the London end, had dropped fully off the road: it would have to be raised up to above rail height and then moved across so that the flanged wheels could be lowered on to the rails. The sweat was already on our brows as we unloaded the equipment - jacks, rams, packing etc.

An appreciative crowd of holidaymakers on the sea wall and platforms watched our efforts as we worked solidly without a tea break in order to beat the heat of the day. The first lift failed to get the wheelset clear of the rail, and so we had to have a second attempt, by repacking under the wheels before lowering and removing the jacks to have another go. This being completed successfully, the next move was to use the rams to align the wheelset over the 4'8 1/2" gauge, and then gently lower the loco back on to the road.

During this operation the 'Scillonian', the steamship that plied the route from the Scillies to Penzance, berthed at the nearby jetty and began to unload its cargo of flowers, potatoes and tomatoes. These would be sent forward to the Midlands and London in the first place via 3S15, the 12.25 perishables and parcels service to Glasgow (just as soon as 50014 had cleared access to the rail loading bay).

Once our work was complete and we had cleared up, the foreman told us that we had a couple of hours spare before a suitable path back to Plymouth became available. The sea looked very inviting, and so some of the lads took a swim, while the rest sat on the sea wall eating hot Cornish pasties fresh from the bakers. We all had a good laugh, the local womenfolk wolf-whistling at the sight of railway workers stripped to their underpants.

At 4pm the 'Scillonian' set sail for the Islands and a little later the breakdown train trundled slowly back towards Laira, this time with 50014 at its head. My verdict: a good breakdown, although rather sunburnt.

50041 and unidentified class mate in the Flower Bay at Penzance under dark skys on 31st May 1987. Photo: Brian Daniels

Thundering Fifties

Introduction

This is the sequel to 'Blood, Sweat and Fifties', written in response to the many fellow enthusiasts who have asked me for another light reading book of tales from the depot floor. My involvement with the last three 'celebrity' BR Fifties and those now on preserved lines has brought me into contact with many fascinating people. I sincerely hope that my encouragement and support given on outings from Alresford in the south to Carlisle in the north has given others much enjoyment over the past three years.

As before, your purchase of this book is a direct contribution towards keeping preserved 50149 thundering on in years to come. Thank you for your support.

Have an enjoyable read!!

Mike Woodhouse

Ivybridge, Devon, December 1993.

With thanks to:

My dear wife Valerie; Mr Geoff Hudson; Mr Malcolm Wishart; The Laira team, A,B,C shifts; Mr Paul Furtek.

50033 and 50050 as D433 and D400 stand outside 1-4 shop at Plymouth's Laira Depot. The as built livery with pre-TOPS numbers was re-applied in preparation for the Midland Scot Railtour. 5th February 1994. Photo: Mike Woodhouse

Foreword by Geoff Hudson, Area Fleet Manager Laira T.& R.S.M.D.

The final run down of the Class 50s since 1990 has undoubtedly been an eventful time. I was always aware that the interest in the Class would at least match if not exceed that of the Deltics or the Class 40s. As such I was determined to allow people who are not normally privileged to the intimate details to have as much exposure to the Class as possible. In this sequel to 'Blood, Sweat and Fifties', Mike Woodhouse has managed to capture the reality and hard work in keeping these machines on the road.. He provides a rare insight from the shop floor, of the hard, sometimes unpleasant tasks of maintaining these locomotives, as I am sure some of the preservation societies are beginning to learn. There is nothing glamorous about maintaining Class 50s. It is basically a hard slog, frequently frustrating and which to railway managers has sometimes seemed a bottomless pit into which your budget sunk!

But perhaps I am wrong. In the heart of a true railway man there is something magnificent, almost indefinable, about a pair of Class 50s at full chat, and for many people at Laira that hard work has been worthwhile. At the time of writing we are moving into uncertain territory on the railway, but one thing is certain: the Class 50s will have established their place in history.

First and Last

During my time working at Laira depot I have seen quite a few diesel classes come and go. The Fifties are no exception, and this story is about 50003 'Temeraire'. D403, as it was originally christened, entered service in November 1967. It was sent new from the Vulcan Foundry to Crewe for driving training duties, and became the first of the Class to be loaned to Polmadie (Glasgow). Here it was used for training on the route to Stirling and Perth. The first serious failure came whilst powering the 1505 Crewe-Perth on February 17th 1968, when the B3 exhaust bellows fractured, causing the fire alarm to ring.

At the start of June that year it was returned to Vulcan Foundry for modification. Another first came in October 1972, in the form of the Class debut over the Pennines, with the 2154 Manchester Mayfield-Leeds parcels. Return was on the 1950 Sunderland-Liverpool. Reports a month later suggested it would be the second to move to the Western Region, though this turned out to be a little premature. Transfer in fact came in March 1974, to Bath Road (Bristol), where it was the first on the Western to be renumbered to the TOPS system. In April 1974 50003 set the scene for the next two decades by becoming the first Class 50 to be allocated to Laira. Here is when my involvement begins.

Initially '03 was used for depot training, and then shared duties with other Type 4's - Classes 52, 46 and 47. A large batch of 50s followed suit in moving to Laira that May.

Come 1977 and the Western Region management (via the British Railways Board) made the decision to name the entire fleet. The 'Warship Class' tag never caught on, being overshadowed by the previous Class 43 hydraulics on the Western Region. The individual loco names, though, soon proved popular. It was my privilege to affix two gleaming nameplates (cast at Swindon Works) to '03 on May 9th 1978, this being the 26th Fifty to be named at Laira. 'Temeraire' - an old naval name, best known for its second bearer which fought at Trafalgar. In the 1960s Class 43 D851 (also Laira-based) had carried this name.

The new 'Temeraire' came to grief at 2300 hours one bitterly cold winter's night in January 1979 just down the line from Laira at Plymouth station ('North Road', as it once was). The loco had recently been outshopped from Doncaster Works in standard Rail Blue livery, but with white-rimmed lights fitted into the sealed-over headcode panel. Anyway, on this night the frost was already thick as '03 waited to take over 1A03, the night sleeper service from Penzance to Paddington. At last the train came, but as the Fifty set back onto the stock it was unable to stop in time, and suffered serious cab damage. The Laira breakdown unit was called, and it was found that the braking system had iced up. As a result it was back to Doncaster Works again for '03, spending 18 months there this time. The loco emerged on September 19th 1980 refurbished and sporting the 'large logo' livery (the second of the Class to receive the new paint scheme). A week after the official release date it worked back to Western Region metals on the 0950 Edinburgh-Plymouth, taking over from a Deltic at York. From Bristol to Taunton it was joined by 50043, on a test run from Bristol Bath Road.

On August 18th 1982 '03 made another foray north, with the 0700 Bristol-Leeds and 1237 Leeds-Cardiff parcels. The next time up this way the loco was not under power, being towed for Doncaster for an engine change. The power unit had failed in service on February 2nd 1984, with the piston liner and cylinder block being damaged and the crankshaft having to be scrapped. With a new 'heart' in place '03 left 'The Plant' on April 6th. Six weeks later and it was given the honour of working the first down 'Torbay Express', the 1035 Paddington—Paignton, complete with headboard.

A year after the previous trip to Doncaster came the final visit for 'Temeraire' under the existing maintenance regime, this time for treatment to underframe fractures. It was off works at the start of May 1985. From 1986 there was a radical change of policy, with CEM ('cost effective maintenance') introduced, whereby Laira became a 'Level 5' depot and thus responsible for heavy maintenance, instead of BREL Works. A major part of this programme was the F exam, and much of my time at work was spent in the team undertaking these exams on the Fifties (see Page 39). These were done for Network SouthEast, which under sectorisation had taken over responsibility for most of the fleet. After the mechanical side invariably came the repainting into the now-standard Network livery. 50003 was in the NSSA pool, for working the Waterloo-Exeter route. In the New Year of 1988 it was stopped at Laira for what was to be the final F exam given to the Class.

By this time we had ironed out all the snags that came with undertaking heavy maintenance! '03 was released to traffic on May 9th, having lost its black-roof version of the large logo livery (applied in 1986), and instead sported the revised version (darker blue and modified corner styling) of the NSE colour scheme.

Three years on and the rundown of the fleet was well under way, but with unclassified work still permitted for the time being. '03, for example, received new radiator banks in May 1991 to alleviate high water temperature problems. However, on June 14th 'Temeraire' suffered a main generator failure, and was dumped in the milk dock at Clapham Junction. Eight days later 50017 towed the dead loco home on the 1815 Waterloo-Exeter; and on July 13th 1991 50003 was officially withdrawn, along with 50007 and 50048.

The clock of time had come full circle as, two days later, I performed the last rites by removing the nameplates which I had put on all those years ago. Farewell 'Temeraire'.

It was a sad day as '03, berthed in No.5 road, was made ready for the cutter's torch. I had been one of the first fitters to work on the Fifty at Laira, and now I was one of the last. At least the parts donated by '03 would keep the others running. Power unit No.6957 would bark no more, and we also removed 16 cylinder heads, 16 pistons and liners, 4 traction motor blowers, the ETH auxiliary generator, the radiator fan motor, radiators, telephones, batteries and so on. The rust had taken its toll on all of the cab sides, with the 'mouseholes' even being marked and labelled.

'03 was then moved to Ocean Siding, between the mainline and the Plym estuary, for storage with its classmates. However, this gave BR a serious trespass problem, with people crossing the busy mainline, and so all the withdrawn Class 50s were moved to a siding in the nearby Tavistock Junction yard. The locomotive was by this stage a sorry sight; badly vandalised, with windows smashed and cab fittings destroyed as it stood among the weeds and bushes.

The end at last came in April 1992 when, in the company of 50048, it was towed to MC Metals in Glasgow for scrapping.

This was truly a First and Last story.

Summer Working: Exeter 1985

It is August 1985 and I am rostered for a spell at Exeter stabling point, servicing locos on the night shift while the regular fitter is on leave. This also gives me the opportunity to ride fifties to and from Exeter, the 1840 Penzance-Bristol on the way up, and the 0702 Exeter-Penzance back.

Sunday evening on the 18th finds me at Totnes station ready to go, while on the hillside above Totnes Castle is all lit up. In rolls 50008 with the string of old mark 1s and mail vans that regularly form the Bristol train. I make my way up to the driver to hitch a lift to Exeter. Soon the whistle is blown and 'Thunderer' roars away up Dainton bank. There is plenty of wildlife beside the track, with rabbits caught transfixed by the headlight beam. At the summit Dainton Box is closed, and all the semaphore signals are showing green lamps. We dip down the other side towards Newton Abbot, and then alongside the Teign estuary, where it is high tide and the night shore men are out with their lanterns. Teignmouth and Dawlish see many holidaymakers get off; maybe they have been for a day out at Newquay, St. Ives or Looe. At Starcross the rows of colourful lights on Exmouth esplanade twinkle across the waters of the Exe. '08 now accelerates hard, up to 95mph through Exminster, before power is shut off to coast into Exeter. The mark I's swing and rattle through the points outside St. Thomas. The lovely old triple-gantry semaphore here has been replaced by a single colour—light with a 'feathers' route indicator. Tonight it shows a yellow, plus the white feathers lit to send us into Platform 6 at Exeter St. Davids.

On Christmas Eve 1988 50003 'Temeraire' is captured on Exeter Stabling Point. The loco clearly needs repairs to it's No 2 end multiworking cable. Photo: Carl Looker

We clatter over the point work and draw to a halt at 10pm.

7am Monday morning, the night's work is done and now it is homeward bound. The 0702 stopper to Penzance is a booked 50 turn, the loco being one I have serviced on the stabling point. It is thus to my advantage that it behaves itself on the way home - I'm tired and ready for bed! Today it is 50026 that waits under a clear blue sky: another hot summer's day is in the making.

Departure is from Platform 3, the stock again being ancient mark 1s. The train is lightly loaded, most people probably commuters on their way to work in Plymouth.

St. Thomas is our first stop, where a solitary person is waiting to board. 'Indomitable' waits impatiently at the green signal, engine revving and with the ETH on. Off come the brakes and '026 powers up, exhaust barking as the 0702 heads west into the sun. Both the driver and I pull down the sun visors. The red sandstone cliffs behind the Dawlish sea wall reflect the bright light as a Class 47 comes towards us with 3A27, the 0625 Plymouth-Old Oak empty newspaper vans. This time it is low tide on the Teign estuary, and grey herons and sandpipers are feeding on the mudflats.

With only 175 tons behind, the fifty makes light work of the climb past Stoneycombe Quarry to Dainton Tunnel, where power is shut off for the coast downhill to Totnes. The station there is reached at 0750; nearly bedtime for me. On the platforms the station staff are busy watering the hanging baskets and feeding goldfish in the pond. For most people another day is just starting.

As for me, I wonder what fifties will be around tonight?

For the record, these are the locos I travelled on and worked on at Exeter that week:

	1840 Pz-Br	0702 Ex-Pz	Serviced
Sunday	50008	50026	08840 31203 33061 33062 45056 47015 47539 50018 50026 P465 P466
Monday	50026	47602	31231 33053 37101 45056 47589 47602 50049 P463 P465
Tuesday	47602	50011	31231 33034 33050 45003 47358 50011 50024 P466 B472
Wednesday	50011	50009	31203 31231 31273 33034 33050 47014 47142 47233 50009 P463 P465 P480
Thursday	50009	47611	31209 47083 47280 47560 47611 50001 P465 P470 B472
Friday	47560	50041	31209 31273 33043 45016 47142 47238 50002 50041 P463 P470

Silent Night

10pm on Thursday May 21st 1992; darkness has fallen on a quiet, routine scene at Laira. My turn is almost over, and I have put my tools away and am writing up the worksheets. Then comes a call over the tannoy calling me to the supervisor. The 0915 Glasgow-Plymouth HST has failed on Rattery Bank: a rescue mission must be launched!

No class 47s are on shed. D400 and 50033 are under repair, and I have just finished my shift by signing off on 50007, which is being prepared for a railtour in two day's time.

The decision is taken: 'Sir Edward Elgar' will have to have to go the assistance of the stricken HST, and I am to accompany the loco. I collect my hand lamp and tools, then remove the battery charger and start up '07 ready for the off. The loco is parked on No.4 road. A driver comes over from Plymouth station and makes a final brake test in readiness for the service run.

The engine is powered up and we ease out to the dummy signal at the exit.

Plymouth power box gives us our instructions, namely to run out to South Brent and await a linesman. The message from the HST driver is that he has stuck near the site of Tigley signal box, but our driver does not remember the route when the box was operational.

Off we go running light, along the river estuary and up the 1 in 42 of Hemerdon Bank.

Out in the darkness to our left are the southern foothills of Dartmoor. Soon we come to a halt at the colour-light signal at South Brent, where there is a twenty minute wait before the lights of a road vehicle pierce the black night. The linesman unlocks the facing points on the ground frame and instructs us to proceed wrong-line to the failure. The railway here is signalled for bi—directional running, and the AWS sounds as we pass the signal. No sooner are we clear of the up line when a Res-liveried 47 overtakes us with the Plymouth- Newcastle postal. It's a very strange feeling to be travelling up the down line, especially as it is pitch dark. Owls hoot and nocturnal creatures scamper about to add to the eerie atmosphere.

Sounding its horn 'Sir Edward' enters the single bore of Marley Tunnel, the headlight illuminating the rail as we progress at a steady 20mph. Trees overhanging the cutting at the east end sway as the loco pushes air out of the tunnel. Nearly there. The engine is allowed to idle as we creep down the grade: it is no easy task sighting a failed train in the lightless Devon countryside, where there is no straight track, just curve after curve. Not a word is spoken, our eyes are glued to the rails ahead. I can't help thinking, what if we are running too hard, and the HST is hidden round the next corner? The dryness in my throat is not helped by the whoosh of the Plymouth—London postal (another Res 47) as it comes up from behind and bowls past on the adjacent set of tracks.

No sooner has the last van of the postal cleared when I see a white headlight across the corner of a field ahead. We stop to judge the distance still to go, and then explode the detonators put down to protect the crippled train as we inch forward. I can hear the crunch of ballast under '07 as the 117-ton loco noses up to the HST power car. The Glasgow train has stopped in a wooded section on a bend, making it even blacker, if that is possible. We get out and greet the driver and guard, who are relieved to see us stop safely.

The camber and curve of the track is such that connecting the emergency tow bar is not going to be easy. Using my hand lamp I wave the driver of '07 on; he edges the Fifty up until it is nearly touching the HST. Off comes the nose cone of the HST and the heavy tow bar is lifted into position. The pin drops into place first time – lucky! The mandatory brake test is made, and then '07 prepares to restart the two dead power cars and seven Mark III coaches on the steep gradient. With a blare on the horn the driver opens the controller right up. No.2 end cab is leading, and the headlight cuts a penetrating beam into the night.

Fortunately the rail head is dry and there is no wheel slip. 2,300 amps show on the gauge as the best of English Electric lifts the stricken HST up Rattery, the bark of the 16-cylinder CSVT engine echoing far across the slumbering countryside. We head for Plymouth and home, releasing the queue of trains blocked back behind us. Within half an hour we pass the bright lights of Laira, and shortly roll into Platform 7 at Plymouth North Road. It is around about midnight: 'Sir Edward's' good deed is done. We are not required to pull the failed set back to Laira, so after detaching we run back light to the depot. I can now finally sign off duty, and the real star of the evening, 50007, can rest awhile on No.4 road before greeting its fans on the railtour on Saturday morning.

The Lifting Road

It's that time of year of year again when, due to staff holidays, I have to spend a fortnight on the lifting road. At Laira we have specific men employed on this duty day in and day out. They have special tools and know all the snags associated with the job.

The task before us on this occasion is to make good two Class 50s using bits from a third, which would then be sent to Doncaster for Classified overhaul. 50040 was the one due for Works attention, and when it arrived after being towed dead from Old Oak we are able to make a start on returning 50018 and 50042 to traffic. To complete the picture, '40 also has to receive the bogies off 50048 before it could be despatched north. This operation was to continue round the clock, including weekends.

'Leviathan' is berthed on the jack (No.1) road, and our first job is to release all the components from both No.1 and No.2 bogies. All eight bodyside lifting brackets are then put in place, allowing the loco to be lifted high into the air off its bogies. Next they are wheeled out and replaced by those from '48, brought in from storage in the sidings. Outside on the oil road '18 and '42 are each awaiting a new wheelset, as the flanges on those fitted have worn down to below scrapping size. 'Triumph' is first to be treated, with its No.2 (middle) wheelset on No.1 bogie needing to be replaced. Of course, being in the middle it was hardest to get at. '42 is placed on the jacks and lifted once No.1 bogie has been released (No.2 bogie staying with the loco). Working under the suspended Fifty it is time to remove No.2 traction motor and release the spider with the aid of a forklift. A spider, in case you are wondering, is the four-legged box-girder frame mounted on the bogie, on the top of which sits the loco body. It is supported underneath by coil springs and dampers. Anyway, with the spider released the next stage is to push No.1 bogie back under and lower '042. The components surrounding the No.2 wheelset can now be removed, namely the brake rods, horn stays and front bow girders. The bow girders between No.'s 1 and 3 wheelsets are shackled up, as is the bogie to the bodyside. Now we are ready to take the lift again, except that this time both bogies are being raised. The aim is to leave the defective wheelset behind, which can then be taken away to have its axle box removed (this can be re-used on a good axle).

The process is repeated many times, as summarised below. Hopefully you can appreciate why it is such a time-consuming business!

Remove both bogies from 50040.
Refit with two ex 50048.
Remove No.1 bogie from 50042.
Remove No.1 spider.
Remove No.2 traction motor.
Refit No. 1 bogie.
Remove No.2 wheelset, unserviceable.
Refit with a serviceable one ex store.
Remove No.1 bogie and place aside.
Remove spider from No.1 bogie ex 50040.
Remove No.2 traction motor.

Refit No. 1 bogie ex 50040.
Remove No.2 wheelset, serviceable. `
Refit No.2 wheelset unserviceable ex 50042.
Refit No.2 traction motor.
Relit No.1 spider
Remove No.1 bogie ex 50040 and place aside.
Refit No. 1 bogie on 50042.
Remove No.2 wheelset, unserviceable.
Refit No.2 wheelset serviceable ex 50040.
Remove No.1 bogie.
Refit No.2 traction motor
Refit No.1 spider.
Refit No.1 bogie
50042 - Loco complete.
Bring in 50018 with No.2 bogie facing west, i.e. needs turning on the 'triangle' — an 08 tows the loco round Laira, Mount Gould and Lipson Junctions.
Remove No.1 bogie.
Remove No. 1 spider
Remove No.2 traction motor.
Refit No.1 bogie.
Remove No.2 wheelset, unserviceable.
Refit No.2 wheelset ex spare, unserviceable.
Remove No.2 bogie and place aside.
Remove No.2 bogie ex 50040.
Remove No.2 spider.
Remove No.5 traction motor.
Refit No.2 bogie on 50018.
Remove No.5 wheelset ex 50040, serviceable.
Refit No.5 wheelset ex 50018, unserviceable.
Refit No.5 traction motor
Refit No.2 spider.
Remove bogie ex 50040 and place aside.
Refit No.1 bogie on 50018.
Remove No.2 wheelset ex spare, unserviceable.
Refit No.2 wheelset ex 50040, serviceable.
Remove No.1 bogie.
Refit No.2 traction motor.
Refit No.1 spider.
Refit No.1 bogie.
50018 — Loco complete.

'F' Exam Programme

It was during 1986 that the CEM - 'Cost effective maintenance' — programme was announced. Certain of the larger depots on British Rail were to become 'Level 5' maintenance bases, and carry out heavy overhauls which previously had only been undertaken at BREL works.

Laira was one of the depots chosen, and subsequently was allocated the 'F' exam work on the Class 50s. This took the place of a Works visit after about four years in traffic.

Previously we had only undertaken as high as an 'E' exam, the two-yearly service. Not only was some of the work new to us, but we also had to demonstrate that each stage of the operation was being done in the most cost-effective manner.

When all this became known, I was asked to set up a programme to ensure the smooth running of the 'F' overhauls. My suggestion, called 'Operation Laira Care', was based on a flow chart containing some twenty 'boxes', or separate operations. The idea was to save time by moving the loco around as little as possible during its stay; in fact, it only ought to be berthed twice. The 'boxes' were as follows;

BOX 1: If the loco is in running condition at Laira, start up the power unit and check all fuel, oil, water and exhaust systems as per instructions. Make a note of any modifications and rotten body panels that will require repair. Pass this information to the Controlling Officer. At this stage the power unit is valued on the basis of engine hours accumulated, and perhaps earmarked to resurrect a failed classmate (with main generator flashover damage, often as not).

BOX 2: If the loco is not a runner - as was usually the case with those based at Old Oak - make a detailed list of all faults and missing parts. Often a loco assigned for the 'F' exam would be robbed of parts in order to keep others in service.

Next, remove compressors and exhausters for bench testing. Renew all parts as required, for example compressor cylinder heads and commutator brushes, and check and clean items such as valves and motor commutators.

BOX 3: This involves taking out all items that need to be completely renewed, and for which the loco is berthed on No.6 road stop blocks. Remove all roof panels end to end, and then the air filters. Remove main fire bottles, exhausters, traction motor blower motors, air receivers, air brake valves and feed cut-off valves. Remove radiator fan and motor, all radiators, and release the power unit. Remove the ETH generator. Remove all floor plates throughout the locomotive and radiator corridors; not forgetting to mark up all the parts, of course! Remove cab seats, main doors and batteries. The electrical cubicle is to be fully overhauled in situ. Draw back the loco under the 50-tonne hoist, and lift out the power unit. Finally, remove the fuel lift pump.

BOX 4: Now the loco is dragged round to the steam cleaning pit for a thorough scrub, end to end, inside and out. Once certified clean enough it is taken to the bogie road.

BOX 5: Lift and remove both bogies. Remove large main air receivers. Remove drawbars and main screw couplings. Remove all buffer beam fittings (hoses, etc.).

BOX 6: Clean underframe, paint all conduits and colour code the pipework.

BOX 7: Replace drawbars, screw couplings and buffer beam hoses. Replace underframe air receivers and compressors. Renew all traction motor flexible muff couplings.

Install overhauled bogies and a new set of batteries. Work on the underframe is now complete and the loco can return to No.6 road.

BOX 8: Examine all conduits through the loco. Test the fire conduits and nozzles and carry out a full tire test card, excepting the main fire bottles, which are replaced new.

BOX 9: Repair all rotten or damaged body panels. Carry out any modifications, if required, while the loco is still gutted.

BOX 10: Repaint the loco end to end, including the inside compartments, but not the cabs. Replace all floor panels. Renew all oil, fuel and coolant hoses. Replace the fuel lift pump and all overhauled air receivers, radiators, traction motor blower motors and trunkings, exhausters, plus the fire bottles.

BOX 11: Pull back the loco to under the hoist and lift in first the new power unit and then the ETH generator.

BOX 12: Fit out both cabs. Reassemble air valve, cut off valve and feeds. Replace all filters throughout the loco.

BOX 13: Now comes the repaint of the bodywork into the livery of the owning Sector's choice.

BOX 14: All roof panels fitted end to end.

BOX 15: Repaint the cabs and fill the washer bottles.

BOX 16: Fill the loco with coolant and lubricating oil. Prime the fuel system.

BOX 17: Start up the loco and carry out a full test procedure on each system — mechanical/electrical, power, brakes etc.

BOX 18: Final adjustments.

BOX 19: The loco emerges into the open for the driving controls to be tested.

BOX 20: A loaded trial run to Exeter or Penzance. If this is passed then a sticker is put in each cab, which reads: 'Operation Laira Care', with date of completion.

These boxes were not fixed in terms of running order. For example, if No.6 road was full then the loco could go to the bogie road after boxes 1 and 2 were complete, even if this meant putting the old bogies back on temporarily for moving around the shed. As each part was removed it was to be cleaned and painted, and then stored in racks by No.6 road ready for reassembly. Rubbing down for painting could begin from Box 1. Work sheets were issued only as and when the parts became available. Parts for the next loco in line were ordered half way through the current CEM.

The new scheme was put into operation for a contract from Network SouthEast, which required 22 locos to be treated for the 'Thames and Chilterns' and 'Solent and Sarum' operating pools. First to arrive was 50026 'Indomitable', from Old Oak, in early September 1986. My procedures were put into practice, and the work progressed smoothly. By the afternoon of October 2nd 1986 all was complete,

and the loco was posed outside, resplendent in the sunshine in its new NSE livery. Laira's first CEM level 5 'F' exam had been a success. Standing in the doorway of the shed, camera in hand, I felt heartened by what the Laira team had achieved, and pleased that my system had worked without a hitch.

During the first few 'F' exams, however, delays became apparent due to the air receivers not returning from the outside contractors in time. As a result it was suggested that an extra set be introduced into the flow system. 50006 'Neptune' was selected to be the donor loco, and so was dragged over from the scrapline for the removal of this and other valuable parts before being consigned to Vic Berry's scrapyard in Leicester. Meanwhile, over at Doncaster Works, they too were out shopping Fifties for Network SouthEast. From July 1986 to March 1987 'The Plant' dealt with 50035/037/044/002/048, 'Ark Royal' famously returning to the WR in grey undercoat as they did not have the livery drawings or colour specifications.

After '26 we at Laira had 50034, and then 50018 and 50025. Next came the depot flagship 50007. In theory it should have reverted from its special GWR—green to the standard NSE livery, but the Network Manager himself gave permission for the paint scheme to remain, so as to mark Laira's workmanship and dedication to the Class 50s. The next in line also retained its original livery, 50046 being released on May 11th 1987 and keeping its large-logo colours until the end of its life. July saw a modification to the standard livery with 50050, which was painted in a darker shade of blue and with vee-shaped cab side markings instead of the previous wrap-round pattern.

After 'Fearless' and 50028 there was a lull in the workload while discussions took place at Derby about the proposed Class 50/1 Railfreight conversion. The 'F' work team were given 50044 for a 'D' exam in the meantime, and we wondered whether 50043 or 50049 would be chosen as the prototype, as they were the next two down on the shopping order. The regeared Class 37—specification bogies were ordered in readiness from Crewe Works. As the saga continued the odds shifted in favour of '49, since 'Tiger' was now waiting for an overhauled power unit from Crewe to complete its CEM, and 'Eagle' would also need re-engining. 'Defiance', though, had a half-life power unit, thanks to a visit to Doncaster for derailment damage in 1985. Railfreight were hoping to carry out trials with their 'new' loco in September, and what with many staff on their summer holidays the depot would be at full stretch.

Thus it was that 50049 was selected to become 50149, the tenth Laira CEM, with 50043 as number eleven and getting the standard NSE look. Through August and September 'Defiance' took on a new guise, and many top-brass officials came down to Devon to inspect the progress. Details of painting and drawings for the decals, nameplates and arrows were posted in the cabs. By September 22nd the Class 50/1 was unveiled and made its first light test run. The next day it became derailed, and after this was put right, the loco promptly wrote off its power unit · but that's another story!

50043 as expected then had its 'F' exam, being released on November 10th, and was replaced by Old Oak's 50030. 50024 followed, the last of the OC machines to be treated.

This was due to be finished by Christmas 1987, but in fact was completed on December 16th. Thirteen done — and not a single one had needed to return for rectification, a credit to the standard of work carried out by the depot staff.

During the run up to Christmas a new Area Manager came to Laira. I had worked for this man many years before, when he was the Chargeman Fitter at Old Oak, and knew that he was a stickler for detail, especially in the cabs and on the bodyside as they were on public display. With my mates we made the decision to give 101% attention to this on 50027, the fourteenth CEM. So it was that about 8am one morning the new boss paid us a visit on 'Lion'. He came into No.2 cab and found that every nut, bolt and screw was in place, the relabelling was complete, and there were not even any paint runs to be seen.

After a very thorough look round he congratulated us on the state of the cabs and bodywork. I gave a wink to one of my mates, who replied with a grin and a thumbs-up sign.

But, a manager being a manager, he then went into the engine and found 20 jobs needing attention. To be fair, they were mostly on the Crewe power unit! Indeed, Crewe Works were having a difficult time with the Class 50 engines (having recently taken over from Doncaster in this work). The power units were not always up to scratch, and on being run up would present us with a fair amount of additional work.

'Lion' was released three days before the New Year, and it was announced that the three remaining 'F' Class 50s would be 50001/017/003. They had to be complete before the end of the financial year on March 31st. 'Dreadnought' was returned to service on January 21st 1988, and 'Royal Oak' on February 15th. Then in came 'Temeraire', for the final heavy maintenance ever to be undertaken on a Class 50. '03 was suffering from severe rust around the cab sides, windows and lower skirt, the holes being labelled 'mouseholes', and the task was set about re-plating and filling the affected areas. For some reason the amount and location of rust varied a lot between locos.

By March 9th 'Temeraire' was ready for a light trial run, sporting a lighter shade of NSE blue for some reason. Another episode in the Class 50 story was coming to a close.

What would I do from now on? My procedures had worked well with the Fifties, and so when Laira was awarded the contract to refurbish 15 Class 37s the 'Laira Care' treatment was extended to this 'G' exam programme. So it was that l spent the next sixteen months working on these 'growler' beasts.

Friday Rendezvous

Friday morning: the Tories have won the General Election, and for me an epic 48-hour rail journey is about to begin. After several difficult weeks preparing D400 and 50007 for their railtour run up the WCML to Carlisle the time for action had come. The first stage is to run light engines up to Stewarts Lane depot in London. My mate and I book on a 1430, where the Fifty duo are basking in the afternoon sunshine on No.4 road, taking on fuel and water. We report to our production manager for the final briefing. I listen with a feeling of excitement and trepidation as the instructions are given. These include to remember the 'live' third rail on the Southern Region, and so watch where you are walking — especially after dark. On the London Midland no climbing on the roof to fill the header tank or radiator, as the 25KV overhead line has only a minimum 12" clearance above the top of the loco. Keep an eye on the water and temperature; and make sure the drivers stick to the 75mph speed limit!

Some mechanical and electrical spares are stowed on board, including CU1, CU3, CU4 and CU6 fuses; all flexible buffer beam hoses; high pressure and low pressure fuel pipes; rubber clips and tape; lamps; and windscreen wipers arms and blades. There are even line drawings of the electrical, air and braking systems. The locos are given a final check: oil, coolant, and fuel levels; windscreen washers and wipers, horns, driver's safety device, all OK. The driver performs his checks, including the stationary brake test.

Someone shouts "good luck!". The two mighty English Electric engines burst into life. They both take power together and so we move out to P191, the exit dummy signal. It is 1520, and '07 No.2 cab is leading the way. Plymouth control gives the road, and 1,000 amps is enough to edge the Fifties through the point work at Laira Junction and out onto the mainline. No turning back now!

The AWS bell sounds all clear as we cruise through Tavistock Junction Yard, the field divert being taken as we reach 60mph at 1,500 amps. On through Plympton and the line visibly steepens as the sharp climb that is Hemerdon Bank begins. The driver opens up to Notch 6 to maintain a steady

60mph, but with 5,400hp on tap there is plenty in reserve.

Near the top a yellow signal trips the AWS siren: the light engine special is to be put inside at Hemerdon Loop to allow service trains to pass. By 4pm the 1535 Plymouth-Paddington and 1544 Plymouth—Derby have cleared the road and we are let out, only to be held a few miles on at my home town of Ivybridge. As we wait for the section to clear, Dutch liveried 37038 passes on a down engineer's train. Another short advance and halt, at South Brent, where lambs frolic in the fields and the embankments are strewn with gorse and primroses. Onwards through the rolling Devon countryside until at last Exeter is reached; at 1655, a little behind time. A change of crew and a change of marker lamps, as D400 No.2 cab will be leading on the leg to Salisbury. The Fifties roar up the bank to Exeter Central in fine style. At Pinhoe a black cat dashes across the track in front of us: hopefully a good omen! There is a wait in the loop at Honiton to cross the 1315 ex-Waterloo, and so I have a good look round the engine room of D400. With the aid of a hand lamp I check the header coolant tank gauge; turbocharger pressures; the exhaust systems for blows or overheating; the power unit for leaks; fuel, coolant and oil levels; the engine governor oil level and pressure; battery charge rate; the commutation of the main, auxiliary and ETH generators; plus keep an ear out for unusual noises. Back in the cab I must make notes of anything untoward for examination back at the depot. My mate does the same in '07.

RES—liveried 47717 is late with the train from the capital, and we have to wait again at Chard Junction. 47579 in NSE colours passes at speed with the 1515 ex-Waterloo, and then we are clear to Yeovil Junction, where Southern upper-quadrant lattice semaphores can still be seen. It is now 1810. An electrical failure at the level crossing at Sherborne means we have to be flagged away by hand for the stage to Templecombe. Here we pause to let 47709 power the 1615 ex-Waterloo out of the single platform. Near Gillingham it is the turn of a ginger cat to dart across the rails and get a blast on the horn, while at the station loop we greet 47702 on the 1655 ex—Waterloo. Tisbury Loop and we cross 47701 on the 1715 ex-Waterloo. The intensity of the service on the largely single line is very apparent.

Our Laira fifties have had no problems by the time we roll into Salisbury, with darkness falling. The new depot for the Class 159s looks nearly complete. A driver from Waterloo replaces the Exeter man; he will take us up to 'The Lane' and then across to Clapham Junction for stabling overnight. He is a cockney sparrow and a right chatterbox, and keeps us amused with his tales all the way to London. An interest of his is studying maps, and he tells us that an Exeter—Waterloo train at one point has the loco in Hampshire, the middle coaches in Wiltshire and the tail in Dorset: how's that for boundary crossings! At Oakleigh we are told to look out for the llama that lives by the line, but it is too dark to spot anything out of the ordinary.

Our driver friend comments that we have not seen anything other than green signals all the way from Salisbury, and our progress continues at a smooth 60mph. A wood pigeon gets a headache as it hits D400's horn grille on the co-driver's side at Fleet: now I know how these things get bent! Between Fleet and Farnborough is the unique 1½ miles of dead straight and level track, with a line speed 100mph, not that any records will be attempted today. Still nothing delays us, and even Woking fails to interrupt the run of green signals.

"This is most unusual", remarks the driver, "I've not used the brakes once since Salisbury. Perhaps we'd better try them and see." The locomotive straight air brake is allowed to rub on, the needles coming off the stop mark. "Yes, that's OK." As we plunge into London's suburbia the half-hour deficit of the first part of the trip has been all but wiped out. Only at Wimbledon do we get a double then single yellow, and the Fifties engines idle for the first time since Salisbury. We pass through the station with speed falling to 30mph, to the accompaniment of several cameras clicking. The white feathers on the signal ahead light up to direct us onto the sharp curve of the freight-only line to Point Pleasant Junction. After the massive yard of Wimbledon depot, where the tower lights beam down on the EMU fleet just like daylight, the trackbed is shared with London Underground trains. Late night commuters get the rare sight of a pair of Fifties heading towards Battersea.

We grind our way between ranks of back-to-back houses on a 15mph curve to join the line to Wandsworth Town. This is all new mileage to me, but soon the more familiar territory of Clapham Junction is reached. "This is where you will stable tonight", remarks our driver. The tracks ahead wind and twist over viaducts; somehow we thread our way through to Stewarts Lane, which has to be reversed into. Once the dummy comes off we ease into the depot confines, parking up against 56061 and with 73005/006 alongside.

I climb down with our water can for tea making, and observe four Class 33s and four Class 73s stabled. There is also the withdrawn 73111, cannibalised and covered in graffiti.

Inside the servicing shed there is no third rail to be wary of. As I return with the fresh water our driver is asked to move up, as 50007 has been serviced and now it is the turn of D400.

The time: 2230.

This time tomorrow we'll have been to Carlisle and back!

Twenty minutes later and the locos are ready. We have a last look round, checking the bogies, jumpers and lamps. Fuel, oil and coolant have all been topped up, and so we retrace our steps to Clapham Junction yard. The Fifties are run into the old station bay and shut down. After screwing down the handbrakes we have a nightcap with our jolly cockney driver, then say cheerio to him at midnight and prepare to kip down in the locos. Tomorrow will be our marathon day: the Area Fleet Manager will be on the footplate, and all eyes will be fixed on the Laira specials. Let's hope 'Sir Edward' and D400 behave themselves.

Shap Here We Come!

5.30am: dawn steals over Clapham Junction Yard. My mate and I wake cold and stiff in the cab of 'Sir Edward Elgar'. '07 and D400 are fired up in preparation for train 1Z38, 0820 Waterloo to Carlisle!

As the locos build air pressure we check the engine rooms. The cooker is on in readiness for toast and coffee. A wash in cold water removes the last traces of sleepiness, and the sun is just about to burst over the horizon. It promises to be a fine day ahead. Already some early travellers are on the move. The basic checks done we have our breakfast, and see 73207 on a 'Gatwick Express' and 47636 on a rake of ten empty NSE mark II coaches — the stock for the tour.

7.00am: our driver has arrived, and once he is ready we ease forward to the dummy signal. On phoning Waterloo control he is told that they are only aware of light engine movements being booked: sorry, no railtour to Carlisle today! In consternation we retreat to the siding, and with the aid of the mobile phone kept on '07 contact Laira and Swindon for instructions. At last the right computer keys are pressed and the Class 50 railtour is back in business. Twenty minutes late we head for Waterloo, the sun well up now.

Hundreds of cameras are clicking as we sidle into Platform 12 at Waterloo, the new International station taking shape to our left. Next we shunt across to Platform 11, in which stands our train. What with two locos up front this is too long for us not to foul the starting signal. We find our AFM (Area Fleet Manager), Mr Hudson, and escort him to 50007, where he is introduced to the driver. Even the Boss has come to ride the fifties to Carlisle! 0835: the final brake test is complete, and we are ready to go. The handsignalman liaises with the power box over the intercom, and waves the green flag to give us the road.

Our marathon journey is underway. 1,500 amps are taken to lift the train into motion, and the pair of gleaming fifties stride confidently through the maze of lines and points. There is a glimpse of Big Ben between the skyscrapers. We gather speed, passing the concrete track bed for the 'Eurostar' trains of the future. Through Vauxhall and Clapham Junction, where we are routed onto the Windsor line, then immediately we get a red signal. The driver leaves the cab and walks back to the guard. Heads appear from every window of the train.

It transpires that we have left Waterloo without a tail lamp, and so one is hastily brought over from Clapham Yard.

The bark of eight English Electric exhausts echoes around the buildings as we reach 60mph on the approach to Twickenham. I am in D400 and my mate is in '07, which is leading on this leg of the journey. It's time for a look round the engine room of D400, which is very warm, but there is no sign of overheating or exhaust blows, and oil pressure is steady at 60lbs. There is a booked stop at Staines, and here I swap places with my mate, to join the AFM in the leading cab. Off again, with diverts taken at 42mph (1,100 amps) and 60mph (1,500 amps). Our Southern Region driver is a little heavy on the controls, his frequent notching up and down causing the electrical contactors to flash in their cubicle.

Many photographers are in evidence by the lineside, and the horn is often sounded.

Large gas holders mark the approach to Reading and the Western Region, and we get a double yellow with direction feathers to take us into the station. A Laira HST set heads for Paddington as we draw to a stop. More railtourers pile on, and 'Dennis the Menace', a New Street driver, takes over at the helm. He asks for a timing sheet as no instructions had been available at Reading.

19 minutes down we head out onto the mainline, and can at last make some real progress at a steady 75mph. Inside '07's engine room the oil pressure is 65lbs. Again there are no leaks, and the contactors are quiet - what difference a sympathetic driver makes. I re-enter the cab just as the driver points out the cab of a Deltic in a garden adjoining the line; somewhat out of place in Great Western territory! Our passage along the Thames valley is interrupted by the AWS siren tripping, prior to the fifties being diverted from the Down Main to the Down Relief line. The point work is one of the new 70mph turnouts, a marvellous engineering achievement. After the whole train has snaked across three lines power is applied again. 37146 plus 37521 are noted at Didcot East Junction, and the Great Western Centre is about to open for the day. Five more minutes are lost as a Class 47 with the Mark I Pilkington stock is allowed ahead of us on the line to Oxford.

A cup of tea is in order and so the cooker goes on to boil the water. When it's ready I have to squeeze

50007 leads 50050 (as D400) passes Nantwich with the Carlisle Fifty Farewell. Photo: Rob Catterson

through the loco to the leading No.2 cab with the boiling kettle, not to be recommended when the train is jigging along at 75mph!

Tea for four is taken as we race towards Leamington Spa. The brake leaks on as we slow for a speed restriction over a crumbling viaduct. Once through the station our driver notices that the signalman has set the wrong route ahead, and so we stop at the green light.

Driver Dennis get out and phones the Bobby, who says he has been given no instructions about the tour. It is explained that our timing sheet shows that we are to make for Birmingham New Street via Coventry, and so the signal changes to red. Three minutes or so pass before the signal can be reset for the proper road, then at last we are able to take the single—track Coventry line at Avenue Junction. The tour is looped at Kenilworth to await a southbound HST, a Craigentinny set. It is not long before we see Coventry power box and turn sharp left to join the WCML, the bogie flanges screeching round the 30mph curve. In the station we take the through road, and are given priority over a Euston-Birmingham electric. Likewise at Canley a local Class 310 unit on a local service is looped for us to pass. We hustle along the mainline under the wires, then slow for the dark and dripping tunnel that heralds arrival at Birmingham New Street.

1115: the platforms are thronged with hundreds of railfans. 'Dennis the Menace' leaves to be replaced

by Saltley crew, and I swap with my mate to ride D400. Soon we are away, still a little behind time, but the echo of the exhaust beat of the fifties in the tunnels and dank cuttings is music to the ears. A pilot is taken on at Wolverhampton for the route to Shrewsbury. D400 is up to 1,700 amps and 70mph by Oxley sidings, by which time we're deep into unspoilt LMR countryside, with plenty of upper—quadrant semaphores still around.

At Madeley Junction 58005 is sighted coming off the Ironbridge branch with MGR empties from the power station, and at Wellington the signal arm remains firmly horizontal until we are nearly upon it, causing our locos to take 1,700 amps of power to regain momentum.

After a look round D400's engine room, Shrewsbury is upon us. We negotiate the sharp curve of Abbey Foregate Junction and note 31155 and 56038 stabled by the station.

1,900 amps as we pass the majestic signal box, only eight minutes late now, and head out into rural Shropshire on the North and West route to Crewe. A policewoman is controlling the photographers at the Nantwich level crossing. A few more minutes and the train eases on the approaches to Crewe. Past Gresty Lane signalbox and the rows of scrap Classes 08, 31 and 47; past the ranks of stabled locos on Crewe Diesel depot. With horn blaring we roll into the famous station: the fifties are on their old stamping ground now.

Our Shrewsbury pilot gets off, and the Saltley driver is joined by a Preston man. The enthusiasts throng around the locos, and even two of the station staff show an interest.

They used to work on the Class in their LMR days, and one comments "I never thought we would see these again". The stewards have a busy time shepherding everyone back on board 1Z38, and then the station supervisor blows his whistle and we are on the move again. Photographers are even on the roof of the signal box at the north end of the station.

50017 'Royal Oak' is glimpsed in its new home of the Crewe Heritage Centre. It is as yet untouched, only having arrived from Laira a fortnight ago. Another check inside D400: again everything is fine. 90146 flashes by with a southbound freightliner. We are romping along the WCML now, just like the doubleheaded expresses of the early 1970s. 78mph is easily reached at Warrington. At Winwick Junction we leave the mainline to skirt the famous Vulcan Foundry at Newton-le-willows — the birthplace of the Fifties. It is their first visit back in many a long year, and - who know? - it may well be their last. People by the lineside give the thumbs up. Everyone, from toddlers to grandparents, has come to witness this historic moment.

Speed drops to 30mph as we grind against the check rails through Earlestown station. I walk through the engine room of D400 to the No.1 cab, where opposite me in '07's cab are the AFM and my mate. Parkside West and Golborne Junctions allow us to rejoin the mainline. I am enjoying myself on this tine run. Both fifties are performing faultlessly. Wigan Springs Branch depot has old Class 20s and new Class 60s stabled in the sidings, and an ex-Laira Class 142 DMU, still in its chocolate-and-cream livery, passes by beneath us at Wigan Wallgate. Another reminder of home is found at Preston, where stabled in the bay is 47824 'Glorious Devon'.

Again the platforms are thronged with hundreds of people who have come to see the Laira twins. I swap over to ride '07. We thread out past the site of the splendid overhead gantry where blue and unnamed D407 had been photographed when brand new, almost 25 years ago. Our driver remarks that he has not been over Shap on a Class 50 since the early 1970s, when Preston men were heavily involved with the Class. At a steady 75mph we head north, alongside the M6 for part of the way. A photographic stop is booked at Lancaster, and I ask the driver to stop short on the long platform so as to prevent the multitude of photographers from spilling out onto the track ahead. The film processors must be making a fortune today!

The tension mounts, as this is the last stop before the ascent of Shap. Once everyone is safely back on board the horn is blown and the gleaming 50s lift the ten-coach train effortlessly into action. It has turned quite overcast now. Past Morecambe Bay we race, through Oxenholme, and into the Westmorland Fells. The gradient begins to steepen. Shap here we come! 1,750 amps gives us 78mph as we forge up the picturesque Lune gorge, spring mountain rivers flowing like silver. Tebay, Greenholme; 50007 and D400 storm on, reliving the excitement of doubleheaded Anglo—Scottish expresses of two decades ago. It's memory time. Cars are parked in every available spot. Our fifties put on a fine show for the spectating crowds. Then, at 1519, a cheer goes up in the cab as we breast the summit, some 916 feet above sea level. Down the other side at 80mph, and time for me to have an inspection of the engine room again. Penrith is passed in a flash, and in no time the AWS siren sounds for the run into Carlisle. A group of railmen are on the flat roof of the signal box by Upperby depot taking pictures. Many more people are on the station itself to witness this piece of history. Yes, the railtour had made it to its destination.

A quick check of oil, fuel and coolant levels shows all is OK, but our driver has instructions to take the locos to Upperby for safe keeping - and also our well-earned lunch break. LNER Pacific 'Blue Peter' is on shed, but not in steam. The staff there welcome us, but say they don't want the Fifties back! Some horror stories of working on the Class are regaled to us. Tea is made, photographs are taken, and then after 20 minutes it is time for the return journey, featuring (of course) the ascent of Shap from the north.

Back on Carlisle platforms there is a presentation ceremony, with the publisher of 'Rail' magazine handing over a cheque to the AFM and the NSE West of England Route Manager. The money is to help keep the last three celebrity fifties running. As we wait for the off at 1655 the Boss is badgered into allowing the locos a crack at achieving the magic 'ton': 100mph, just like in the good old days. Sportingly he agrees, but only on the coasting downhill of Shap. The signal winks green, and amid a blaring of horns we begin the 371 mile trek back to London Waterloo.

During the photocall at Penrith a passenger tells me that D400 is losing coolant. An anxious check of the radiators and engine finds the gauges reading full and radiator fan working properly, so it must have been an overflow after being topped up at Carlisle. Underway again, pounding up Shap, and all eyes are on the quarter-mileposts and stopwatches. Again the stiff climb presents no difficulty to the locos, and then they are allowed to run downhill. For once the spectacular scenery is not given a thought. In our cab the speedo registers 102mph, at 900 amps, for quarter of a mile. Everyone is delighted: the Thundering 50s have scored a century for probably the final time in the history of the Class under BR ownership. It is a moment to savour.

We head south through a variety of English landscapes and into night. The Preston crew tell us they have had an enjoyable day out, and hand over to Saltley men. Engineering works mean a long, slow crawl into Crewe, but still many ebullient railtourers come up to congratulate us.

As always, we are held in the tunnel on the approach to Birmingham New Street. I look out as the exhaust dislodges soot from the tunnel lining. The lights from the carriage windows make shadows on the walls.

Coventry, Leamington, Banbury, Oxford. An uninterrupted 75mph down the Thames valley to Reading, and then back onto Southern metals. A final look round inside D400 at Staines.

The lights of the Capital beckon, and soon after midnight we draw up to the hydraulic buffers on Platform 12 at Waterloo. Our marathon day out is complete: both locomotives have performed faultlessly, and the many enthusiasts go home happy.

The new day will see the running of the London Marathon, but for us it is a case of getting some well-earned kip and a ride back to Laira 'on the cushions'.

Thunderer's Last Exam

As readers may already know, 50008 'Thunderer' has always been my favourite fifty.

Today is November 21st 1991, and I am privileged to be on duty to perform the last ever 'A' exam on both '08 and 50015, prior to their final working for British Rail. This will be in two day's time, in the shape of a railtour from Paignton to Newquay and then Bristol. Funds raised will go towards keeping 50033 in traffic.

My first duty is to receive the 'A' exam worksheets from my supervisor. On them is a list of 26 items, which cover the whole loco. '08 is berthed on No.6 road stop blocks with '15 immediately behind. 'Valiant' is having the background to its nameplates painted black, to give it the textbook Departmental 'Dutch' livery.

With my hand lamp and oil sample bottle, I commence the examination by entering No.1 cab and checking all the safety items: detonators, shorting clips, fire extinguishers etc.

I also check that nothing new has been entered by drivers or travelling fitters into 'Thunderer's' repair book.

Next I go down 'B' side, first looking at the header tank coolant gauge in the radiator compartment. Then it's into the engine room. By removing the dipstick I can now check the lubricating oil.

The engine governor oil and lay rub couplings also get inspected. Continuing down the narrow

Thunderer in the Laira blue livery waits its next turn of duty on 2nd February 1991. Photo: Carl Looker

internal gangway, I check both exhauster oil levels, and then emerge into No.2 cab. Once again the safety items have to be gone through carefully. With the battery supply on I press the 'start' button. 08's engine rumbles and bursts into life, settling down to a regular tick over. A pall of blue-grey smoke hangs above the loco. After monitoring the exhaust emission by eye I reenter the engine room to examine the power unit for gas, oil, fuel and coolant leaks on both 'A' and 'B' sides. The oil pressure is noted, and a specimen of oil taken for the analyst.

Outside once more, going round all the marker lamps, headlamps, windscreen wipers and washers, to make sure they are all working correctly. Then back into No.2 cab to check the ammeter for battery charge. I carry out a full power, brake and DSD test, and then do the same again in No.1 cab. 'Thunderer' can now be shut down, so that I can take a look below solebar level.

Numbers 1 and 2 bogies are scrutinised for tyre and brake block ware, also for any loose or defective parts. The sump oil levels of the left- and right—hand compressors are tested. All nose—end buffer beam hoses, screw couplings and lifeguards are looked over to ensure they remain in adequate condition. Finally I get onto the roof to make sure that the roof hatches are securely pinned down. All 26 checks are now complete. The exam has taken two hours to do, and now I can hand over the work sheets to the supervisor, who will then authorise the loco for return to traffic. Many thousands of man—hours on many hundreds of exams have now come to an end. In two day's time 50008 will have run its last mile in traffic, bringing to a close another successful Class 50 career with British Rail. It will then join its stalemates on the scrap line, to await preservation or the cutter's torch - but that's another story!

My feeling is one of sadness; but somehow I feel sure that 'Thunderer' will one day pound the metals again.

Update: The good news, is of course, that 50008 still thunders on, now owned and operated by Hanson and Hall, it's mainline certification means it is regularly seen at locations across the UK.

'The Minster Marauder'

Early November 1992, and once again I am called upstairs at Laira to see the Production Engineer. Not - of course! — for a carpeting, but to learn of another Class 50 challenge. A railtour from Eastleigh to York requires a pair of Fifties onwards from Bristol - and I have been chosen to accompany them. My mate and I are to travel up by service train on the Friday evening, stay the night in a hotel, and then pick up the Fifties at Bath Road depot ready for the early departure.

The day soon arrives, and we book on to find a Laira crew preparing 50007 and 50033 for their excursion to the outer reaches of Yorkshire. An HST whisks us up to Bristol, and we walk over to Bath Road to make our acquaintances. Next we find our hotel, and over a late meal discuss the forthcoming trip. A 6am call is requested, and a taxi ordered. No chance of breakfast being provided at that time of day! Arrangements are made for our meal tomorrow night, including a contingency plan in case we are late back.

A warm and restless night passes before the call comes through. By 0615 we are outside, tools and hand lamps at the ready, waiting for the taxi. The intrepid railtourers will already be on the way up from Eastleigh. A change of shift is due at Bath Road when we arrive, and so it is rather quiet. We walk down to the servicing shed, just as '07 and '33 roll in light engine from Laira. The Shed Supervisor meets us, and offers to fuel and water the fifties while his men change over. This is done while I check over the locos. Soon after 7am all is ready for us to move off shed and work 1Z42, the 0725 Bristol to York special.

'Sir Edward' will lead the way on the run north. Quite a crowd of enthusiasts has gathered to take early pictures. The stock — a rake of maroon Mark Is and IIs - is already in the platform. Our driver for the journey arrives, saying he has come from Birmingham New Street by rail taxi - a Class 37 light engine! The ETH is switched on and the usual brake test made. A 'Thumper' DEMU draws up at the adjacent platform, this being the first leg of the tour. Its occupants pour out and soon the station clock shows it's time for the off.

A Paddington-bound HST is let out before us, but then we discover there is no Guard to work our train. Half an hour elapses before a spare man turns up; he is greeted by cheers from all down the platform. A quick second brake test is made for him, and then the 'Route Available' light winks on and we power out from under the famous vaulted roof. All seems well until leaving Wickwar Tunnel, when the ETH suddenly drops out. I make a reset but am unable to make it stay on: something is amiss with either the locos or the coaching stock. My mate and I resolve to take a look at the Cheltenham stop: the buffet car crew will soon be anxious for more hot water. The jumper leads are duly inspected and my mate now rides on 'Glorious'. The horn is sounded and we forge away, ready to do battle with the Lickey Incline. 37719 is in the Bromsgrove oil terminal at the foot of the bank, and then as the Fifties bellow up the stiff climb, to the appreciation of scores of lineside observers, I take a look inside '07's engine room. The 16 cylinders are pounding away, giving their all, but the oil pressure is a steady 60Ibs, the exhaust pipes are not overheating, and there is no sign of any leaks. Back in the cab, though, I find that the ETH has dropped out again.

As we breast Lickey summit the controller is notched back. New 25kv masts have sprouted out to Barnt Green as part of the Birmingham Cross-City link to Redditch. A crew change is booked at New Street, and I take the opportunity once more to examine the ETH connection between '07 and '33. Soon we are away, having made up some of the lost time.

The troublesome ETH stays on, so it must be an intermittent fault on the electrical circuit.

Our new driver used to take Fifties down from Brum to Paddington, but now was in the link servicing Didcot Power Station with Class 56 and Class 58-hauled MGR trains.

Saltley depot is passed to the right, and on shed is ex-Laira 37417 'Highland Region' (presumably also ex—Scottish Region!). Close to here is where InterCity proposed to build a replacement for New Street, called 'Birmingham Heartlands'. At Water Orton East Junction we diverge from the mainline onto the Nuneaton line. The driver offers me a cup of tea, an offer no railwayman ever refuses! To my surprise, though, it is Earl Grey with no sugar. What a different taste: not my sort of cuppa. The track hereabouts is very rough, due to mining subsidence, and in places there are 20mph speed restrictions. Daw Mill Colliery is seen on our left, this being a regular supplier of Powergen at Didcot. The problems with our on board electricity continue, as the ETH fails again. Our next tactic will be to isolate '33 and let '07 provide the heat alone. A single yellow slows us for the sharp curve onto the West Coast Main Line at Nuneaton. 158852/842 accelerate by heading for Birmingham. Still on a single yellow we crawl through the station, to the consternation of an old couple sitting on a platform bench.

After only a mile so heading south on the WCML we diverge eastwards at Midland Junction, and power up for the climb to Hinckley and on to Leicester.

This is the last pickup point, and a Pilotman is taken on for the run to Sheffield via Toton. He turns out to have worked as a secondman on the fifties out of Carlisle when they were new. Indeed, he had been involved with the running-in turns with locos fresh out of Vulcan Foundry. This would most likely be his last ride on the Class.

A reminder that the wheel turns full circle came in the form of new Class 60s 60006 and 012 resting on Leicester stabling point (**Update:** now UK Rail's depot). Up the line at Loughborough we speed at 75mph past the Brush Falcon works where they were built. None are visible in the compound there today. The massive cooling towers of Ratcliffe-on—

Trent power station send steam into the atmosphere as we head for Toton Yard. On Toton depot just about every type of Railfreight diesel class can be seen, including withdrawn Class 20s. 58035 comes towards us from under Sandiacre bridge with a rake of MGR wagons, and then we notch up for the run north to Chesterfield.

Time for another look round the engine room of 'Sir Edward'; everything is still fine. A pair of Metals Class 37s pass us with the famous crooked spire of St. Mary and All Saints Church in the background. At Dore South Junction '07's ETH drops out: at least we now know who the culprit is. Sheffield station is packed with railfans. Time for a crew change, and we say goodbye to the Leicester pilot and Saltley driver (plus his Earl Grey tea — now cold!).

Their replacement is a York man who only drove DMUs for Regional Railways. In fact he had only handled a Fifty twice before, when delivering them back to the WR on the 0950 Edinburgh-Plymouth after refurbishment at Doncaster Works. He gets the railtour on the move alright, but the single yellow at the tunnel mouth causes the AWS to trip and for a moment he can't find the reset. I just manage to get to it before the brakes go on.

With a bit of assistance he soon gets the hang of working a 'real' loco again. As we head out of Sheffield the new Meadowhall shopping complex and even newer light-rail network are visible. At Swinton Junction the indicator directs us onto the Mexborough line, as the advertised route via the Bolton-on-Dearne is closed. The ETH, which I had put on again at Sheffield, trips once more. Oh well, time for a cup of tea — thankfully of the Ty-Phoo variety this time!

It is not long before we reach Doncaster and the East Coast Main Line. 321902 in the fetching West Yorks Metro livery of buttermilk and red is parked in the Leeds bay. Out on the level and flat of the ECML the Fifties can stretch their legs once more, but at nothing like the pace of the Class 91 that whisks by at 120mph, the vortex of air rattling the co-driver's window. The run into York commences as we pass the now-lifted Dringhouses freight yard. With the massive girder structure of Holgate Bridge in view the controller is eased back, and then we glide beneath it to be greeted by the majestic sight of the vaulted York station and the towering spire of the Minster beyond. We run into Platform 9 and come to stand. I make contact with my mate in 50033, and we decide to hang fire with the ETH jumper trouble until after our perambulation of the Harrogate circle, when the locos will have to run round.

A Riding Traction Inspector joins us for the circle, and we show our footplate passes and make our introductions. He is keen for us to depart, so as to slot into the public services, and gets onto Control with his radio. Soon 1Z42 is underway again. I get talking to the driver about 50A, the old York steam and diesel shed, as it was in the early 1960s.

A schoolmate of mine had gone there as an apprentice fitter in 1959, at the same time as I started at Old Oak Common. We used to make exchange visits and go for footplate rides, on the Class 40s and unnamed green Deltics in my case. Our driver today was able to recall my friend of long ago.

The signal is off for us to leave the 25kv wires at Skelton Junction, where a Class 56 on MGR heads south on the mainline.

We head west into open Yorkshire countryside, complete with upper-quadrant semaphore signalling: unspoilt railway scenery. Hammerton Station has its own crossing keeper, who comes out to open the gates for us as we are brought to a stand at the starter signal. We hand over the Poppleton-Hammerton single line token, and then power up only to come to an abrupt halt. Thinking there had been a failure my mate and I dive into the electrical cubicle in '07, but in fact it was only because the crossing keeper had forgotten to give us the next token. The drama over, we continue to Cattal and on to Knaresborough, where the beautifully situated viaduct offers superb views.

Our driver points out what is claimed to be the only thatched cottage in West Yorkshire.

A pair of fifties on Knaresborough Viaduct, what a photographer's dream. Slowly we proceed, with the only traffic seen being Pacers and Sprinters - home from home for our driver.

A photostop is made at Harrogate. This is my first time here, and I am impressed by how well the station buildings blend in with the dignity of their setting. A Class 144 unit heads for York under the now overcast sky. We forge south for Leeds, the line twisting uphill through woods. Many Pacers come to grief on this section during the leaf-fall season, but there is no sign of wheel slip from '07 and '33. After Horsforth there is a four mile descent at 1 in 100 into the built-up conurbation of Leeds. A long viaduct carries us across the River Aire and the Leeds to Liverpool canal. In the station 91024 waits on a rake of Mark IVs with a Kings Cross service. The route ahead is signalled green and we pick our way out through the point work.

Now we are heading east once more.

Neville Hill depot contains a couple of brand-new NSE Class 165s, here for weekend tyre turning. A check of the engine room is made; the ETH is still tripping, but otherwise 'Sir Edward' is in the best of health. Colton Junction sees us rejoin the ECML,

The crew and support team in conversation beside 50007 at Leeds Central Station on the return leg of the railtour on 7th November 1992. Photo: Mike Woodhouse

and in a few more minutes we rumble under Holgate Bridge into York for the second time.

An ex-works Railfreight 90024 is deputising for a Class 91 propelling a London train as our two fifties run round the stock. 'Glorious' will be leading on the way home, and as the ETH fault is definitely on '07 we should now be alright for the rest of the journey. With a shade under 300 miles completed so far (and 261 still to come), the locos are shut down and after checking the coolant we too take a short break. We are already looking forward to our steak supper back at Bristol.

At 1520 our new driver, a Nottingham man, restarts the duo and makes a brake test.

His only previous contact with the Class 50s was their occasional use on Birmingham to Nottingham freightliner duties. Everyone is on board and the Guard is able to wave us off at 1532. At Church Fenton we take the Castleford line, then negotiate a sharp left to Curtsyke Junction and thence to Knottingley. This is colliery country, the track badly affected by subsidence. 30mph is a normal maximum for the 122-tonne Class 56s on the MGR trains.

At Knottingley I recognise a professional video producer friend of mine shooting some film, even though the light level is very low. The depot there, nestling in between the triangle of lines, contains many Class 56s taking a weekend rest. Now we venture down the Askern line, which has never seen a Class 50 before. The rollercoaster dips in the track are very noticeable: no wonder there are so many permanent way slacks.

Shaftholme Junction brings back onto the ECML after this interesting detour. As we canter down to Doncaster I take a look round the insides of '33. It is a little smoky, enough to makes my eyes water. We are held outside Doncaster for first newly—named 91007 'Ian Allan' and then 91026 to pass. This makes us about twenty minutes late. Another detour is made at Black Carr Junction, by way of Gainsborough and Lincoln. It is getting dark now, and Lincoln Cathedral is illuminated proudly on the skyline. It's one more memory to savour of the last days of the Fifties. Another is the 16 level crossings to negotiate on the freight-only line from Boulton junction around Lincoln and then on to Newark!

Soon after Newark we pass from ER to LMR metals, and steadily retrace our route along increasingly familiar tracks until Bristol Temple Meads is safely reached.

Once again the Laira Fifties have done us proud. They will spend the night on Bath Road before running light to Plymouth tomorrow. In the meantime, it is 10pm and we are keen to get stuck into our steak supper.

Hope and Glory

When Edward Elgar wrote 'Land of Hope and Glory' in 1901 I bet he never thought that one day he would have not one but two railway locomotives named after him! Well, there have been moments in my railway career when the 'hope and glory' have made it all worthwhile. One such episode is undoubtedly the fortunes of Laira flagship 50007, formerly 'Hercules' and now 'Sir Edward Elgar'. This story will relate some of those happenings.

Let's turn back the pages of history to the days of the Great Western Railway. Never one to miss a trick, the GWR paid tribute to the Elgar family by naming Castle Class 7005 after Sir Edward, and basing it at his native Worcester (shed 85A). During my time as an apprentice at Old Oak Common in the early 1960s I recall working on this particular Castle, having to remetal bearing bushes for the side connecting rods. Today, in 1993 I am still involved with a locomotive that bears the famous composer's name.

On January 20th 1984, when plain old 'Hercules' was indistinguishable from the rest of the Class, 50007 failed at Kensal Green whilst working 5S61, the 0605 Old Oak carriage sidings to Paddington empty stock. The reason was power earth faults and overloads.

After repair at Old Oak it was kept on restricted workings, but on the 26th failed with the same problems on 1A66, the 1813 Paddington—Twyford. That was the end of the line for 'Hercules', as the decision was taken to ship it down to Laira for repair - and repainting and renaming into the bargain.

'07 arrived home behind 47159 on the 31st, and was back in service on local duties by February 2nd. Six days later the depot was ready for the transformation work to begin.

Off came the nameplates, and the loco was rubbed down ready for the new livery. On the 12th the bodyside was painted in pre-1945 GWR green, and next day the roof panels were done in black. The 14th saw the bogies painted, after changing No.3 traction motor, and the buffer beams given a coat of red paint. Next came the lining out, and then the cast brass name and numberplates were fitted. The cabs were painted grey on the desks and cream on the bulkheads, and the tyres given white rims. Never had a fifty looked so smart!

Platform 1 at Paddington station on Saturday February 25th, the 50th anniversary of the composer's death, and 50007 was in the limelight for its renaming ceremony. The crowds gathered, and with plenty of pomp and circumstance Simon Rattle - conductor of the Birmingham Symphony Orchestra and a godson of Sir Edward - made a speech and pulled the cord to reveal the new name. '07 was booked on the 1215 Oxford and return, and then the 1807 through Elgar country to Worcester. Unfortunately, the fifty only got as far as Royal Oak on its debut trip before No.1 traction motor failed, and so thereafter had to run on just four motors. This meant that due to the lack of field weakening speed could not exceed 60mph, with consequent loss of time. An attempt was made during the brief stopover at Oxford to get all six motors going. Gradually power was applied on departing with the 1415 to Paddington, but soon the overload tripped and the offending motor had to be isolated again. There was nothing for it but to declare the loco a failure on arrival at London, and so there was no Worcester run on this occasion.

From then on the new-look 50007 became a 'VSL' (Very Special Locomotive) featuring on many special duties. For the next ten years the Laira staff applied gallons of Brasso, turtle wax and elbow grease, not forgetting to retouch the white-wall tyres, and so the green machine stayed in pristine condition. The first special working was with the VSOE Pullman stock on March 19th, in the form of a Paddington-Torquay trip for a camera company. On the 24th it revisited its former home of Crewe with the 'Border City' railtour, and April brought visits to Marylebone with the 'Capital City Transfer' and North Wales with the 'Conway Crusader'.

As well as regularly working railtours, there were appearances at Open Days. 1985 was the 150th anniversary of the GWR, a perfect excuse for an assault on the nostalgia market. 'Sir Edward' visited the jamborees at Canton (Cardiff), Landore (Swansea), Laira and Old Oak Common (plus the Stewarts Lane 125 celebrations). On April 7th '07 came to the rescue of the ill-fated GW150 steam special, by working the 1800 Plymouth-Paddington return. July witnessed a similar occurrence, and this next section shows how intensive the use of the VSL was at the time. The loco was allocated to the 1024 Penzance-Liverpool from Plymouth to Bristol on July 6th so that it could star at the Canton Open Day on the 7th.

Next day it worked the 0932 from Cardiff, and back at Laira was immediately serviced for hauling the return leg of the steam-hauled 'Great Western Pullman'. My family and I were waiting at Ivybridge to see the steamer when news came through that it had failed on Dainton Bank. 50045 was detached from the following service and pushed the failure to Totnes, and so '07 had to run light engine to there to collect the train.

'Glory' of a different kind came 'Sir Edward's way at the end of the same month, when a film company put on a 0730 Victoria-Par and 1315 return charter in connection with the filming of 'Minder on the Orient Express', with George Cole and Dennis Waterman.

There was little letup in terms of special jobs in 1986. For example, on March 22nd '07 piloted 50044 as far as Salisbury on the 0548 Exeter-Waterloo, and then proceeded light to the Andover Rail Event. It returned home two days later via the 0954 Salisbury-Meldon stone empties. April 4th and 'Sir Edward' was on the move again, starting with the 1740 Paddington-Wolverhampton. Next day it was tripped light to Chester, from where it left at 1632 in the company of 58040 and 33026, en route to Birkenhead North and the Open Day there on the 6th. July was notable when '07 became the first Fifty over Shap on a service train in over a decade. It worked the 2145 Bristol-Glasgow and 2350 Glasgow-Bristol to/from Carlisle, in connection with the Carlisle Upperby Open Day on the 18th.

Figures are available for the month of August 1986 to show that the loco worked a total of 10,728 miles in 222 engine hours. At no time was it stopped in traffic, with only routine maintenance being required, specifically four 'A' exams, one 'B' exam and two visits to Old Oak for brake block changes. It was a relatively mundane month, with only one VSL turn, but nevertheless the loco ranged as far afield as London, Oxford, Wolverhampton, Bristol, Swansea, Penzance, Paignton and Eastleigh. In summary, it was on Waterloo-Exeter duties on the 1st to the 6th; in the West Country on the 7th; working off Paddington on the 8th-10th; Waterloo 11th-17th; Paddington 18th-21st; Laira for the 'B' on the 22nd; Cannon Street Open Day 23rd-24th; Waterloo 25th—26th, and Paddington for the 27th-31st.

At the start of October 1986 50007 entered Doncaster Works for mainframe crack repair, returning via Stratford on November 7th. Ten days later it powered the 2000 Cardiff-Crewe and 0204 return, the first use of a fifty on the North West route for a fair while.

Into 1987, and in March '07 was out of service at Laira for overhaul on the 'F' exam programme (see page 40). Out came power unit 1H6957, which had given good service, and in went 1H6966. After the Network Director had given dispensation for the loco to remain in GWR green livery out came the Brasso and turtle wax to celebrate. Only the roof panels and cab fronts were repainted at this time. It re—entered traffic on April 2nd, and on May 5th there was some real Hope and Glory when it was chosen to work the Royal Train from Paddington to the Heathfield branch in Devon. This was the first and now almost certainly the only time a Class 50 was entrusted with this type of duty. 1988, and for once '07 was eclipsed by another fifty at an Open Day. Yes, the star of the Laira event in July was Railfreight 50149, which was crested in a ceremony with the Navy. In November the request for 'Sir Edward' to be included in the official Inter City

Charter Unit pool was turned down. Instead, it remained in the newly-formed DCWA Departmental pool. This produced some delights-rather less in the limelight, such as the 0915 Bristol East Yard-Ashton Gate Tunnel inspection train on January 30th 1989, and an Exeter Riverside-Exmouth Junction trip coal working the following day. A week previously it had substituted for a Sprinter on the 1914 Plymouth-Penzance and 2150 return, using Mark II coach 5448, HST coach 42344 and a barrier vehicle. For the most part the loco worked off Bristol and Exeter for the Civil Engineer, including Meldon ballast traffic.

This period ended with the sector changes in May 1989, when '07 returned to front-line duties in the NSSA fleet, dedicated to the Waterloo-Exeter route. A survey of this pool towards the end of that year revealed that 50007 had achieved the best reliability figure - 23,200 miles per casualty. 50050, by contrast, only managed 4,300 miles per casualty!

As the 1990s dawned the withdrawals of the Class began in earnest. On May 6th '07 appeared at Bescot Open Day, yet a fortnight later it lay out of traffic at Laira with main generator flashover faults. By this time it was common practise to rob scrap locos to keep the rest in action, but those vulnerable main generators were always in short supply.

Happily for 'Sir Edward' the extraordinary skill of the Laira electrical staff succeeded in rebuilding '07's genny. A trial run to Penzance with an empty van special was made on June 14th, and the loco then stayed out of serious trouble for the rest of the year.

The green paint was beginning to look a little shabby by 1991, and the spotlight shifted to 50050 and its return to the Rail Blue guise with number D400. I was fully involved with this, including the installation of power unit lH6944. The blue machine made its debut in April on the 0712 Newton Abbot-Exeter, appropriately piloting the green machine. They appeared together again on May 24th, when (as shown on the cover of Blood, Sweat and Fifties) the Laira management arranged a special line-up of the five celebrity Class 50s, 50007/008/015/031/D400 (see the front cover of this book). Not a NSE livery in sight!

Bang!! July 9th 1991 and '07 suffered a serious main generator flashover on the 1315 Waterloo—Exeter near Basingstoke. It was towed to Laira and condemned as a result.

The days of the VSL seemed to be over. 'Sir Edward' was part of the display at the September Laira Open Day, still sporting its brass work. It had been kept more-or-less intact pending the conclusion of negotiations between the Area Fleet Manager at Laira and the Network Manager, which eventually resulted in a reprieve for the fortunate fifty. However, this was to be at the expense of 50046, as 'Ajax' would be withdrawn to provide the necessary parts. So, in November 1991 '07 was towed into No.6 road for restoration to begin, this being designated an apprentices' project. The bogies and power unit needed replacing, and the bodywork required some heavy plating: this would be the last time Laira performed such tasks on a Class 50.

After the power unit swap with 50046, 50007 was tested light engine while still in grey primer. In the pouring rain the loco is seen passing through Totnes on 12th March 1992. Photo: Paul Furtek

0630 Monday morning, and my usual walk to the supervisors office. "Good morning Mike. 50007 on No.6 road, I'll give you some apprentices to start on the rebuild". To my surprise I am joined on the loco by the AFM himself, wearing orange overalls and workman's boots. His comment is that he is to be my colleague for the day - as part of a 'Children in Need' appeal, whereby Management came down to the shop floor to find out what real work was like! So, my 'mate' and I discuss the plan of action. The apprentices would check out all the top auxiliary motors while we went over the electrical cubicle. It all went well and the appeal was a great success. As the weeks rolled by '07 took shape. Power unit 1H6966 was winched out on November 21st, and the engine room and electrical cubicle were then cleaned and repainted. The last job before Christmas was for 'Ajax' to surrender engine 1H6928 and the have it fitted into 'Sir Edward'. Never again would we be lifting a 38-ton Class 50 engine at the depot. Major attention to corroded panels was required in the New Year, especially around the indicator boxes and cab sides. In February '07 was moved to No.3 road jacks for a double bogie swap. Those on '46 had recently been overhauled, and in fact were originally from the Deltic fleet. In return '46 received the scrap sets off '07, destined for MC Metals.

By March 12th 1992 the loco was complete again. In grey primer it went for a light test run to Exeter, even though it was not officially reinstated until the 20th. The apprentice program finished at the end of the month, and then on April 8th the 'hope' of the Laira staff for the continued 'glory' of 'Sir Edward' was put to the test in the form of a loaded trial to Bristol and back with D400 and the TPO set.

All was well, and 50007 returned to pride of place amongst the Laira specials. The first major landmark was the marking of the final day of service by the fifties for Network SouthEast, on May 24th. Out came the Brasso and turtle wax again, and both '07 and D400 were buffed up to perfection, gleaming under the workshop lights at nightfall. 50033 — 'Glorious Network SouthEast' itself - was also be in traffic on the day, but additionally was required on the road the previous day. I asked whether a speed limit of 75mph could be placed on '33 (as was the case for '07 and D400), but that would have been insufficient to keep to the schedule. Alas, 'Glorious' flashed its main generator whilst speeding at 95mph near Basingstoke, and so 'Sir Edward' and D400 were joined instead on the final day by a pair of Class 33s, the previous staple motive power of the route.

In the last 18 months 50007 has been Laira's ambassador, reflecting the workmanship and dedication of the depot staff. For me it always started with an examination of the whole locomotive followed by charging the battery - and a polish of the brass work to finish off. A can of Brasso is even standard part of the equipment in my tool case! Still, whenever and wherever we go with 'Sir Edward' there is always a sense of pride. Railtours have taken the loco far and wide throughout England and Wales, the crowds gathering to see the immaculate green machine. However, the highlight for me personally concerns the loan of the loco to the National Railway Museum at York, in the summer of 1993. All three Laira Fifties were booked on the 'Bishops Triple' railtour on the June 5th, '07 having a one—way ticket of course. My mate and I were to oversee the handover to the NRM, and travelled up the day before on the 1515 Exeter-York HST (Laira set 46). We were booked into the Royal York Hotel, opened by Queen Victoria in 1878, and had an excellent meal in the palm court restaurant, with a harpist playing and the Minster illuminated across the gardens. Back at Plymouth our colleagues would be preparing the three Fifties for their 0215 departure. For once I had no desire to swap places with them! The big day dawned sunny and hot. After a hearty breakfast we began sorting out the arrangements for 50007's entry into the Museum, starting at York station control. The railtour was due in at 1300, and then all three locos would be detached and run to Clifton Sidings, from where 'Sir Edward' would set back into the Museum yard. Next stop was Leeman Road and the NRM itself. Here we met some of the Curators, who explained how the loco would be displayed during the period of its visit. The Head Curator mentioned that there was to be a small handing over ceremony when '07 arrived. My mate and I swallowed hard, hoping that neither of us would be called on to give a speech! Although we joked about it, this certainly added a touch of trepidation to the morning's proceedings.

Back on the station we learnt that the 'Bishops Triple' had been 12 minutes early at Swinton, but then was held at Doncaster to await its correct path. At 1258 the tripleheader snaked into Platform 9 at York, to the usual tumultuous welcome. Our Laira mates were rather weary, but said the trip up had passed without incident. The look on their faces when I said that they were expected to make a speech was quite a picture.

Anyway, at 1330 the Head Curator officially received the VSL, there were handshakes all round (but no speeches from us, thank goodness!), and we all felt a sense of Laira pride. As we departed on 50033 and D400 via the dummy signal at Clifton sidings I looked back to see the green machine bathed in the afternoon sunshine, on display for the world to admire.

There was a sequel to this episode. Some three months later I was summoned to the Production

Manager's office and asked if I would please do the honour of bringing 50007 back home from the NRM. This time the loco would require an examination first, having lain idle for so long, and then it would haul the 'North Yorkshireman' railtour back to Reading. At York we were advised that we would have to run light to Leeds Holbeck for fuel and coolant, the first time a fifty had been serviced at the depot. That evening over our meal we received a message from the Curator of Operations concerning the next day's operations. It would seem strange working inside a museum.

So it was that we found ourselves standing in the Great Hall of the museum: I remember looking round at the fantastic array of railway heritage and thinking how our own 50007 was just one small link in the chain. There it stood, in the company of 'City of Truro', 'Mallard', 'Evening Star' and others. The Curator joined us, clearly a fifty fan (he even had a picture of 50011 on clay hoods hung on his office wall) and supervised as ex-BR Class 02 D2860 towed 50007 outside to the examination pit. Pioneer Class 40 D200 reposed alongside, another fine example of diesel preservation. We conducted a thorough examination of bogies, underframe, engine room etc., and then were able to start up the fifty with no difficulty.

After more checks, and a final cup of tea in the Curator's office, it was time to say farewell to the NRM. Another little piece of history had been made.

Laying a smokescreen over the suburbs of York, our driver gently trundled '07 off to Holbeck, which sadly was due to close in only a few weeks time. 1325 litres of fuel were taken, the coolant topped up, and the windows washed. Then it was back to York to await the tour. Coupled to green 47833 the long trek south began. For 'Sir Edward' it was a return to more familiar duties, and with it the 'hope' of more episodes of 'glory' in the future.

The Road to the Cutter's Torch

This is a sad story for me to tell; though some of my colleagues are very glad to see the back of the fifties! Costly, dirty and awkward to maintain are just some of the (more polite) criticisms levelled at the Class. Thanks to a great deal of dedication and sheer hard work some are still with us, but regretfully many are just a memory from yesterday. This, then, is how the clearout of the fifties occurred: many to the cutter's torch, but a lucky few to keen preservation groups. Some never made that 'final journey' to the breakers yard, having to be cut up into scrap on site and carted off in metal skips. Even the bogies would leave by road for one of the main BR Workshops.

Let's turn to February 1987, when all seemed quiet on the fifty front, with all 50 still in service. Then came the bombshell that 50011 'Centurion' was to be withdrawn in order to provide a test bed for Class 50 power units at Crewe Works. So it was the 'Centurion' nameplates and crests were removed prior to it working the 3S15 parcels to Crewe on February 20th. Once the overhaul of power units ceased, the end was in sight for '11, and finally it was cut up at ABB Crewe by Texas Metals in September 1992.

On the 4th of June 50006 failed on a Waterloo service, and was destined never to work gain. As mentioned previously (page 39), it was heavily cannibalised as part of the 'F' exam programme, and the decision to scrap the loco came in August. The forlorn and gutted hulk was dispatched to Vic Berry's scrapyard at Braunstone Gate in Leicester, having got as far as Bristol Bath Road by Christmas 1987. What a way to die!

Vic Berry's had become a well-known mecca the previous year as the first modern traction graveyard, when a considerable number of mainly Type 2s had arrived for disposal.

To save space they were stacked three high into the sky - a dramatic sight. '06 Finally made it through the gates off the BR siding on February 8th 1988, in the company of 45144. In a matter of weeks nothing except memories remained of 'Neptune'. It had been the first to be refurbished, and now the first to be scrapped. '06 and '11 had been singled out as they had not received treatment for cracks to the mainframe. The only other fifty in this state was 50014, and so it was not really a surprise that it became the third of the Class to fall by the wayside. As detailed in 'Times Past' (page 58), it came straight out of traffic after a busy day on the Waterloo route on October 8th in order to donate its engine to Railfreight experiment 50149. Withdrawal seemed inevitable, but then it emerged that due to a shortage of locos it would be reinstated. However, little work was done, and a change of heart (!) took place resulting in '14 officially bowing out on December 14th.

There was a lull until April 1988, when sister 50013 was written off at Old Oak on the 6th, the victim of fire damage. Two days later 50047 failed on the 1530 Portsmouth Harbour — Waterloo, and subsequently became the fifth of the Class to be withdrawn.

September proved to be an even blacker month, with 50022 going on the 20th, and 50010 and 50038 being condemned together one week later (though '10 was at Laira and '38 at Old Oak). The 'Formidable' nameplates went on sale at 'Collectors Corner' for £690 each — what a bargain at 1993 prices, when £8,000-plus would be a likely asking price! In the last few hours of November 1988 50012 caught fire on the South Devon banks with the empty stock from the 1810 ex-Waterloo. At 10am on January 16th its fate was sealed.

By now Laira was cluttering up with dead fifties, and so contracts were issued for their disposal. In March 1989 I had the task of making safety checks on four of the withdrawn locos prior to their removal to Vic Berry's. In turn they were dragged inside the shed over the weekend of March 11th/12th for inspection of brakes and bogies. 50012/014 were hauled by 50004 as far Exeter Riverside on March 22nd, and then on to Taunton Yard by 31434 the next day, the train running as 8Z40, departing Exeter 1230. 50022/047 followed in 8Z98 to Taunton on the 24th, where the four were reunited. On April 5th 'St. Vincent` resumed its funeral duties by dragging the quartet as 9Z41 to Leicester Humberstone Yard, from where they were tripped into Vic Berry's two days later. Within a month only 'Benbow' remained to be cut up.

Up at Old Oak 50013/038 were joined on the scrapline by 50039, which was pensioned off on June 4th. With ten down - one fifth of the entire Class — several parties were putting in hand tentative plans for preservation. At the time it seemed a monumental task, with saving even one not being a foregone conclusion. Time has shown, though, that fourteen have been saved, and the last three on BR's books will almost certainly swell this total yet further in 1994. **Update:** while 20 were initially saved, currently there are 18 of the class preserved.

The next withdrawal came about in tragic and spectacular fashion, when vandals derailed 50025 on the 2115 Oxford-Paddington as it sped through West Ealing on August 6th. The crash made the national TV news, with 'Invincible' seen lying on its side, its bodywork badly crushed. It was raised and then parked incongruously in a supermarket car park before being taken to Old Oak and hastily condemned. Meanwhile, 50040 was taken out of service as a source of spares, but despite languishing in an extensively robbed condition, survived on the books as 'stored unserviceable' to see in the 1990s.

Spring 1990 saw the withdrawals start once more. 50021 and Paddington crash survivor 50041 were axed at 2130 hours on April 17th.

Then came (or rather went) 50004 on June 22nd, sparking off a spate of slaughters: 50020 on the 27th; 50034 on the 29th (at Old Oak); and then a triple blow of the axe on July 3rd, with 50016, 50035 and the long-stored 50040 succumbing. By this stage Vic Berry's men had visited the London depot and taken away '13 and '38 in skips, but Laira's

The scrapline of 50s at Tavistock Junction in September 1991. At this time it included '03, '36, and '26. Photo: Mike Woodhouse

50010 was cut up on site at Laira by Cooper's Scrap merchants as the locomotive was unfit to move to their facility. Photo: Simon Woodhouse

Lipson No.3 siding had seen long-term resident '10 joined by '04, '16, '20, '21, '35, '40 & '41 — eight in all. 20th to go was 50019 on August 28th, the loco having being painted in a distinctive all—blue livery for the Departmental sector only just over a year previously. 50032/042, from the same pool, joined it on the scrapline after withdrawal on October 10th. 50023 (another DCWA pool loco) met the final buffer stops some five days later.

A touch of mystery surrounded the end of 50009. It was already supposedly withdrawn when on November 16th it was employed to tow dead '32, '35 and '41 to Old Oak, returning light engine. After a final inspection on a day in which South Devon dripped under a heavy mist we read the inscriptions scrawled on the scrappers: 'gone but not forgotten', 'R.I.P.' etc. 'Conqueror' then set off for one final fling. Of its charges, '032 and '041 were destined to be cut up, but 'Ark Royal' was rescued to become the first to enter preservation, and now resides on the Severn Valley Railway.

The heel of 'Achilles' was mortally pricked on December 11th, a day which witnessed half of the Class now gone when 50005 and the first Laira 'F' loco - 50026 - were also dispensed with- Thus only 24 lived to see 1991, but there was no let up in the pace of casualties. The collision—damaged '09 finally fell in January, as did 50044, the victim of the all-too-common main generator failure. On the 16th of that month there were another two safety examinations to make, when '04 plus '16 were sent to Stratford for stripping (going forward from Exeter behind 56053).

February 1st marked the end of 50024, 50028 and 50043, 'Vanguard' having caught fire west of Salisbury on a Waterloo-Exeter service. It was moved via Westbury to Old Oak in a very sorry state to await its inevitable fate. With two sidings at Laira full of withdrawn 50s it was decided to move some more up to Old Oak; but 50048 did itself no favours by failing at Woodborough with the convoy of '28 and '44. After the dismantling of 'Invincible' by Vic Berry; Coopers Metals took over to conduct the London disposals. 50005/024/032/034/039/041 were dismembered around the turntable, their bogies going by road to Doncaster works and the remains by lorry to South Wales for processing. Meanwhile, '21 and '44 were transferred to Stratford for component removal, though 'Exeter' was subsequently rescued to join '35 at St. Leonards. Another consignment for Old Oak was '19 and '23, which had reached Exeter Riverside by September 22nd. They were still there a month later, but had suffered so much at the hands of vandals that it was deemed safer to stable them inside the fence of the car distribution depot. Eventually 'Howe' reached Stratford, but 'Ramillies' left on board a low-loader bound for preservation. Unfortunately, the lorry broke down in the middle of Exeter, causing much traffic congestion, not least it as could not be fixed for several days!

The press had a field day, with many pictures taken of a traffic warden pasting a parking ticket on the 117-ton loco!

April saw large-logo 50036 fall by the wayside on the 12th and 50001 a week later, but the remaining 14 Class 50s soldiered on into the summer without further loss. Until July, that is, when the knives came out to bring an end to the careers of five more. On the 13th, 50003/007/048 were withdrawn in one fell swoop, the first two with main generator problems and the latter with fire and collision damage. Then, 50018 succumbed on the 22nd, and 50027 'Lion' roared its last the next day.

These extra corpses only added to the problem of where to stable DMUs, especially on night duty, and so a movement of seven of them out to Ocean Siding (right alongside the Plym estuary) was authorised. The locos involved initially were '03, '42,' 20, '40, '45, '26 and '36. However, trespass by vandals across the running lines got to the point where they were moved a short distance further up the line, to the somewhat safer haven of Tavistock Junction Yard.

The withdrawals continued apace. Celebrity large-logo machine 50031 was deemed to have scrap wheelsets and so was written off on the 5th, followed by 50049 on the 16th. Exactly two years later 'Defiance' was rededicated in a ceremony at Laira, having been lovingly restored by the volunteers of the Class 50 Society. 'Hood', too, escaped into retirement, as did 'Lion'. By now there was a great of interest in preservation, with many groups checking their bank balances.

September and the start of the leaf-fall season found a job for 50033 - alias 'Smokey Joe' due the quantity of exhaust emitted - in the shape of Sandite duties in Devon and Cornwall. There was no such luck for 50002/017/037, withdrawn on September 9th. This was the state of play for the 1991 Laira Open Day, which will be remembered by the thousands who visited as the best display the depot had yet put on. Certainly it was a grand tribute to the Fifties. 50001/002/007/008/010/017/018/027/029/31/033 /037/046/048/049/050 were on display, with 50003/020/026/036/040/042/043/045 out of sight at Tavistock

Junction. To round off the festivities 'Renown' and 'Ajax' provided an added bonus by doubleheading the 1704 Plymouth-Waterloo.

Next came news of a reinstatement, when the repair of 50007 'Sir Edward Elgar' was authorised, as an exercise for the apprentices: see 'Hope and Glory' on page 48. On the disposal front, another tendering exercise saw the sale of '02, '17, '27, '31, '42, '43 and '49 into private hands, and '01, '20, '26, '36, '40 and '45 to Booth Roe breakers in Rotherham.

50031, 50035 and 50044 all started their second life at St Leonards Railway Engineering on the south coast. Here they were repaired, repainted and returned to working order. Photo: David Keogh

An 8Z40 special was to run early in 1992 to Rotherham conveying 'Dreadnought', 'Revenge' and the latter-day 'Centurion', including barrier vehicles 9466, 9423 and 17131. 47705 provided the motive power, and I was chosen to ride the train as far as Exeter. With no cab windows and on some no cab doors either it was too cold and draughty to ride on the fifties, so I had to pay my respects from the comfort of the Class 47. Then it was the final goodbye, and they left to continue their trip to the South Yorkshire cutting fields.

February 1992 found another clearout underway, this time from Stratford to MC Metals in Glasgow. 31224 towed '04, '16 and '23 for their first visit to Scotland for many years: they would not see England again!

Only eight Class 50s had seen in the New Year, although the Departmental celebrities 50008/015 were stored pending sale. The last large-logo loco in service, 50046, had also built up quite a following, but time was up for 'Ajax' on March 25th when it was condemned in order to provide parts for rebuilding '07. 50029 also bowed out on that day, its power unit having expired a few days previously. With 'Glorious' restricted to special status along with 'Sir Edward' and D400 (ex-50050), this left only 50030 on front—line duty for NSE. Not for long, though, as two weeks after sister 'Renown' had gone, 'Repulse' too met the end of the line, due to a badly flashed-over main generator.

The story of the three remaining special locos has been well documented, and at the time of writing (December 1993) they are still on BR's books. Of the remaining casualties, they have all left Laira, with the exception of '29 and '30. MC Metals bought '03, '18, 37 and '46, enabling them to have a ride over the Settle and Carlisle en route to Glasgow. Preservationists grabbed the rest, all that is but for 'Monarch'. For nearly four years it had rusted away on Lipson sidings, since September 1988 in fact, and not surprisingly was unsafe to travel. Thus it became the only fifty to be broken up at Laira, by Coopers Metals.

Someone had written on its bodyside "Can Mike Woodhouse and Laira please fix this one". Sorry, 'Monarch'.

Class 50s as at December 1993 and now (2022):

Loco   Name   Location   Disposal

50002 Superb South Devon Railway—Sold from Laira. Still at the South Devon Railway.

50007 Sir Edward Elgar BR Still in service. Now owned by Class 50 Alliance—mainline certified.

50008 Thunderer A East Lancs Railway Sold from Laira. Now owned by Hanson and Hall—mainline certified.

50015 Valiant East Lancs Railway—Sold from Laira. Still at the East Lancs Railway.

50017 Royal Oak Railway Age, Crewe—Sold from Laira. Now on the Great Central Railway.

50019 Ramillies Eridge &. Tonbridge Wells Rly—Sold from Exeter. Now on the Great Central Railway.

50021 Rodney Gloucs and Warwicks Rly — Sold from Stratford. Now at Eastleigh Depot.

50026 indomitable Mid Hants Railway — Resold from Booths. Now at Eastleigh Depot.

50027 Lion Mid Hants Railway — Sold from Laira. Still on the Mid Hants Railway.

50031 Hood Fifty Fund, St. Leonards — Sold from Laira. Now owned by Class 50 Alliance — based on the Severn Valley Railway.

50033 Glorious BR Still in service. Now looked after by Class 50 Alliance — based on the Severn Valley Railway

50035 Ark Royal Fifty Fund, St. Leonards — Sold from Old Oak. Now owned by Class 50 Alliance — based on the Severn Valley Railway.

50042 Triumph Bodmin &. Wenford Railway — Sold from Laira. Still on the Bodmin & Wenford Railway.

50043 Eagle Tyseley — Sold from Laira. Cut up at the Blaenavon Railway.

50044 Exeter Fifty Fund, St. Leonards — Sold from Stratford. Now owned by Class 50 Alliance — mainline certified.

50049 Defiance Class 50 Society, Cardiff — Sold from Laira. Now owned by Class 50 Alliance — mainline certified.

50050 Fearless [D400] BR Still in service. Now owned by Boden Rail — mainline certified.

Times Past by Andy Griffiths.

Now a tale from someone on the other side of the railway fence, who is profoundly grateful to Mike and his colleagues who have kept those 'Thundering Fifties' running ....

19.45 hours, Thursday 8th October 1987.

I have just finished the washing up and sat down to watch the rest of the dreadful 'EastEnders' when the 'phone rings. It is a colleague from the Class 50 Society, who has news that makes my chin hit the floor, in true 'Tom & Jerry' style. 50014, which I had spent an entertaining six years pursuing around the network, was about to end its active service.

Not in a few weeks, or even in a few days. No, it had only a few hours left in traffic – the authorities wanted it back at Laira tonight, so that it could donate its power unit to the experimental Railfreight 50149. 'Defiance' had apparently wrecked its own engine at Yatton earlier in the day, and urgently needed a replacement for its official trials in a fortnight's time.

Poor old 'Warspite' had since June been top of the 'hit list' as the next likely withdrawal, due to it being the last of the Class still left in service with untreated mainframe cracks. Hence its selection for the heart transplant, even though the engine had clocked up over 7,600 operating hours since release from Doncaster nearly four years ago, and so was approaching the need for overhaul. But tonight!

Why, my machine had behaved impeccably all summer (admittedly a change from previous years), and even this very morning I had been happily taking snaps as it chugged through the local Devon countryside with the 0700 Waterloo — Exeter and 1218 return.

Somewhat dazed, I consult the timetable and Class 50 diagrams, which reveal that '14 is booked to haul the 1738 Waterloo-Exeter and then retire to Laira with the empty stock. Since the depot must have the loco tonight then it would surely stick to the diagram.

By now it is 8pm, which gives an ample forty minutes to drive to Honiton and intercept the train there. First, though, the tripod must be found, and I start to foam at the mouth when it refuses to reveal its whereabouts. Rachel (my partner) finds it, in the most obvious place of course, and she gallantly agrees to drive from Honiton to Exeter while I engage in a last sample of haulage. I even persuade her to tag along to Plymouth afterwards, to see '14 shunting the empty stock at Laira and shutting its engine down for the very final time.

There is a full moon as we wend our way down the A373 to Honiton. The stationmaster there informs me that the train is likely to be a quarter of an hour late due to a knock-on delay on the single line, and certainly it seems this way (though afterwards I realise I had been reading the Axminster time by mistake). Anyway, the sight of 'Warspite' thrumming to a halt quickly banishes my impatience and the chill from my toes: this is my loco's last passenger working! A posse of skinheads also get on board, then chicken out, only to climb on again at the last moment, shouting "let's go to Penzance and get tickets on the train!" What a good idea, I thought.

'14 promptly powers away, oblivious of its imminent fate. The Guard pursues the skinheads through the coaches, and they are cajoled into alighting at Feniton. Since there are no more up trains this evening it will be a long walk back to Honiton, especially as it is just starting to rain. For the rest of us there is a twelve — mile canter to Exeter Central to savour; and soon '14 is thundering rapidly through the night. Although too dark to see the mileposts, my log shows an average speed of 79mph between Whimple and Pinhoe, and despite a signal slow at Exmouth Junction two minutes are clipped from the schedule into Central. No dallying there means that the fifty ends its last revenue-earning turn at St. Davids only three minutes in arrears. A lively finalé to '14's career, and I celebrate by firing off a bombardment of pictures of the train in Platform 3 and then as it shunts across to Platform 5. 'Warspite's' noble roar echoes around the Exe valley as it runs round the stock before recoupling for positively the last ever thrash over the South Devon banks. A late running HST whines westwards, and I then I notice that there are passengers on board '14's train. It must be relief to Plymouth: what an amazing stroke of luck! The monitor indicates departure is due at 2151 - in other words, in four minutes time. I fly over the footbridge and persuade a ticket clerk on the point of shutting up shop to dish out a ticket on credit card, and then fight my way back through a scrum of people debouched from the Exmouth DMU. '14 is still there, and in fact has to wait, a little longer for another late HST to clear the road. Phew!

Rachel sets off solo for Plymouth station, and very soon the fifty's engine note surges and we do likewise. However, the initial burst of acceleration is not sustained, and we slow to a stop at St. Thomas halt. Although no — one joins or leaves the train it seems odd, even to my addled brain, for a relief to call here. When the Guard comes round a little later all is made clear: this is the scheduled 2151 Exeter — Newton Abbot stopper (to be followed by empty stock to Laira). In my shock I had failed to register this simple fact from either the diagrams or the station monitor; what a plonker! For reasons not entirely clear I had left the camera gear with Rachel in the car, and so not only would she be going on a wild goose (or wild fifty?) chase, but I would be marooned on Newton Abbot camera -less and penniless. What a farce, and a typical, conclusion to my hobby. I might have guessed that '14 would have the last laugh.

All too soon the journey round the sea wall comes to an end, and 'Warspite' shudders to a halt and disgorges its final load of passengers at 2223 hours and 14 seconds precisely.

Standing beside the grubby machine, which glistens in the gentle rain and chunters defiance to the nocturnal silence, I am still unable to comprehend that it really is time for the final credits to roll. After five or so minutes of soaking up the atmosphere (and the typical Devon rain!) the signal winks to green. The driver eases his charge out into murk, to storm the legendary Dainton and Rattery banks alone. I'm left on the wet platform with just my thoughts for company, and a rich store of, memories to savour. Not even the satisfaction of being there at 'The End' could expel the tinge of sadness on waking each morning and knowing there would be no possibility of crossing paths with 'Warspite' today.

Never again would I hear the loco's mighty engine beat - except in 50149. Maybe it was not quite the end after all.

WOODHOUSE WANDERINGS:

The next four stories are about visits to preserved lines; Sometimes these Woodhouse Wanderings came about due to a telephone call asking for help with a preserved Fifty, and sometimes due to visits by the celebrity BR fifties.

1: Mid-Hants Railway

This first story concerns the first ever Diesel Weekend on the Mid Hants Railway. My mate and I were summoned to the Production Manager's office to learn that the Mid Hants had hired 50007/033 for the gala at the end of April 1993. Our duty was to look after the locos while they were on loan. On the Sunday preserved 50031 would also be visiting, and be rededicated in a ceremony at Alresford with members of the HMS Hood Association.

'07 and '33 travel light engines to Alton while we make the journey by road in a BR van. Departure is at 0800 on a rainy Friday, and we make our way east on the A38, A30 and A303, to Ropley, arriving there some five hours later (just as the rain stops). Here we meet the Locomotive Engineer of the Mid Hants, who makes us very welcome, and tells us that our charges have arrived. However, 'Sir Edward' has flat batteries. Not to worry, as the loco is being resuscitated on the home-made battery charger. On inspection, though, this device is found only be trickle charging '07 at about 10 amps: we'll be here all night at this rate! Maybe Eastleigh depot, some 20 miles away, will lend us a charger. The Loco Engineer puts through a call, and the answer is "send the lads over, we will help you out".

Tea is taken in the messroom, along with members of other groups who are preparing their charges for the weekend. Then it's down to Eastleigh, passing the controversial Twyford Downs road scheme, where the traffic is in chaos. Eventually we get through, and find the afternoon shift supervisor at the depot. Overhead, aircraft are skimming the shed roof to land at the adjacent airport. 60003, 47716, 33002 and ex-works 37377 (in 'Dutch' livery) are noted as we walk through the shed to the battery room, where we collect one new battery charger. It will take both of us to lift it into the van. It is still raining on and off as we get back to Ropley. '07 is put on charge, but the 80amps promptly blows the 13 amp fuse. There is only one spare. We try again, carefully surging the charger until it is steady at 60 amps. With one of the Mid Hants men keeping an eye on our loco, we book in to the hotel at Alresford, and l make a call home. Apparently it's turned into a lovely sunny afternoon back in Glorious Devon. The corner of the hotel is where 50021 `got stuck on a lorry transporter last year: there's no escaping these fifties!

Back at Ropley the Class 50s are blocking the station platform and need to be moved into the shed. '07 is put back on charge and both locos checked over in readiness for the crowds tomorrow. One Class 50 that will not be hauling trains is 50027, a resident on the Mid Hants: regretfully it had not been passed by the BR inspector on his visit earlier this week. With everything in order we retire to the hotel for a shower and evening meal.

Saturday morning is overcast, with further heavy rain having fallen overnight. We decide to stock up on fuses, just in case, so call in at the local electrical shop. On being asked for ten 13 amp fuses the man behind the counter shakes his head and said "if it's that bad you need an electrician!". "You don't know the half of it", I think to myself. Then it is on to Ropley, looking forward to our trip on the line 'over the Alps' to Alton. There are lots of handshakes with Mid Hants members and other preservationists, and then we go over to our fifties, which are booked off shed at noon for their first star turn.

'07 and '33 are checked over and tired up. Deltic 9019 is already out on passenger duty, while 50031 (now sporting a black roof) is being polished. The run up complete, our fifties are shut down until ready to go off shed, and the battery charger wheeled away into the shed. Time to make tea. Many visitors are milling round and taking photographs. It is thus all the more embarrassing when at 1140 we climb aboard to restart the locos only to find that the batteries on 'Sir Edward' have gone flat again. Some battery cells must be down. With only quarter of an hour to blast off, the charger is hastily brought out again and — after blowing another fuse - the juice is pumped into the lame batteries. Just before noon it is now or never: the finger is on the start button, and to our relief '07's engine turns. The driver does his brake tests, and we move off shed, prior to running light to Alresford to collect our train.

BR Class 37 37220 (one of my 'G' exam locos at Laira, and now a Petroleum sector machine based at Cardiff), arrives on a passenger train, after which we are allowed out.

At Alresford we come to a stop in the cutting to await the calling—on signal. Sounding the horn we ease forward on to the stock, to the accompaniment of clicking cameras. The two locos reach beyond the station starter signal, and so we have a hand signalman to wave us off after the enthusiastic Station Master blows his whistle. 'Glorious' is leading as power is taken for the climb out of Alresford. Once out into the countryside there are farm tracks cut into the white chalk, fields of yellow rape seed and watercress beds: this is 'The Watercress Line', after all. Ropley is the first stop, a crossing place on the single line. 'Lion' is stabled here. I take a look in the engine room of '33, and then 5,400hp is applied for the 1 in 80 climb to Medsted & Four Marks. The A31 runs parallel to the line, and many photographers cars are parked at the vantage points. At Medsted there is another

crossing loop, and we have to wait for the Deltic to return. Far in the distance I can hear the unmistakable cry of its Napier engines as 'Royal Highland Fusilier' attacks Medsted bank. When it arrives we have to be waved forward by hand, as our train is too long for the loop.

Now we make for Alton, between masses of bluebells along the lineside; nature at its best. The brake is eased on for a 10mph speed restriction over a bridge, whilst the talk in the cab is of whether the run-round spur at Alton is long enough to take a pair of fifties, as a track machine is stabled on the stop blocks. I volunteer to help the shunter by standing by the track machine and guiding in the locos until the buffers touch. Thankfully, the last wheel flange on '07 just clears the point blade. Next I check over 'Sir Edward's' engine room. Nothing to report, but we will leave the engine running just in case the battery cells should play up. On the adjacent siding sits 50026, once the Laira 'F' exam guinea pig, but now requiring a lot of restoration, having been saved literally from the scrapman. 'Indomitable' was bought off Booths in Rotherham, the only example so far of Class 50 having been rescued in this way. It had only arrived at Alton a few weeks ago, and had many cracked windows and graffiti messages scrawled on the bodyside.

It is not long before the LSWR lower quadrant signals (a first for me) are pulled off and we retrace our steps to Alresford. There is a booked two—hour layover here, so '33 is shut down and '07 left to chunter to itself. Tea and sandwiches are taken while 50031 backs onto our stock for the next service to Alton. We make another round without incident, and it is 9.30pm before our charges are bedded down at Ropley along with 50027/031 and we can get away for a meal.

On the Sunday morning 'Hood' is to be rededicated, and the AFM at Laira, the Production Manger and their respective wives are to attend the ceremony. The first duty for my mate (Laira's 'electrician extraordinaire') and myself is to check the specific gravities in '07's battery cells; some certainly are down. Both fifties are examined and the brakes adjusted. Like yesterday, '07 will be kept running all the time. Finger on the start button, and both locos burst into life. A little smoky, but this soon clears. Over the way '31 is being buffed up in readiness for its starring role.

I am in our friend, the Loco Engineer's office, when the Laira party arrives, and introductions are made over coffee. The plan is to run '07 and '33 light to Alton with the Boss and co. aboard, to be followed by '31 on the stock for a special working. After the ceremony we will do a couple of return passenger trips, before joining forces with 'Hood' for a tripleheaded spectacular on the last train of the day. Our driver today is a familiar face, as he had taken

BR's 50033 'Glorious' stands beside The Fifty Fund's 50031 'Hood' which is receiving attention from a group of volunteers at the 1992 Watercress Line Gala. Photo: Mike Woodhouse

us light into Waterloo prior to the Carlisle trip some months back.

All goes well until twenty minutes before the departure of this final working. Sparks are seen coming from the radiator area inside '07, and a quick look reveals that a radiator fan resistance has shorted. My mate and I examine the fuse and CU4 unit, but to no avail.

This means that a very careful watch will have to be kept on the water and oil temperatures now the cooling fan is out of action. The information is passed on to the Laira management, and it is decided that I will ride 'Sir Edward' and switch off the engine if in any doubt about the overheating. Anyway, '31 backs on to us, and we storm out of Alresford amid a barrage of clicking cameras. More than few enthusiasts chase by car to photograph us at several vantage points. Up over the Alps we go, the three preserved Class 50s putting on a fine show. On arrival at Alton, though, '07 is near to shutdown. There has been no loss of coolant, but the oil has got very hot. 'Hood' is detached separately, as there is definitely not room for three in the run-round spur, and put on to lead on the way back too.

For the last time we pull out of Alton. After slowing for the speed-restricted bridge, the locos are opened up for the stiff climb beyond. Up too go the temperatures in '07, their sharp rise soon causing the engine to shut down and AWS and CCBs to trip. On go the brakes and the train comes to a stand. I walk up to the driver and explain that 'Sir Edward' has had enough. With '07 shut down, '31 and '33 power on up the line after the guard waves

his green flag. With evening drawing in we arrive back at Alresford, to complete an interesting and enjoyable weekend. It has been a very successful show all round, well executed by the staff at the Mid Hants. They gave us Laira Lads a warm welcome and we made many new friends.

2: Torbay and Dartmouth Railway

Just after booking on for night duty at 2230 hours I am requested to walk up the now-familiar staircase to the Production Manager's office. At first l thought it was a set-up, because of the time of day, but I make the journey anyway. To my surprise it was for a legitimate reason, namely that Laira had been asked by the Devon Diesel Group to undertake heavy engine repairs on their preserved 50002 'Superb', as it was needed for a forthcoming Diesel Gala. Apparently water had been leaking into the engine sump, and so I and another fitter from 'A' shift were to be hired out to work on '02 at Churston, the location of the newly-opened workshop of the Torbay and Dartmouth Railway. It is explained that we have two days to remove and replace three cylinder heads, pistons and liners: a tall order. The work will take place outside the shed, using a Jones mobile crane for the lifting. During the rest of the night shifts that week a list of all the English Electric engine tools and spares is drawn up, and my mate is selected from the many good upstanding lads of the opposite shift.

Come the appointed day we book on at 0630 and load the lorry, and then head for Churston. It is overcast but dry - thank goodness! 'Superb' is found stabled awaiting its repair, and with it the private line's Shop Supervisor, with whom we discuss the day's work.

Then it's overalls on and we set to work, first opening up the engine crankcase on A and B sides to check the liners. A2, A3 and A5 are diagnosed as leaking into the sump, and so the roof hatches are opened and the coolant drained for the hard work to begin. Out come the heatshields, induction manifolds and exhaust flanges on the three cylinders. Next we remove the three fuel pipes, three oil trays, three rockers and six push-rods, and finally the external pipework and flexible connections from head to cylinder. It takes all our strength to loosen the cylinder head nuts, many of them being rusty. Once all 18 are removed we catch our breath, both remarking that it is going to be a stiff challenge to get it all done in just two days. After all, it's nearly lunchtime already.

The crane is now used to lift out the three cylinder heads, and they are put down beside '02. Next we bar over the engine to enable us to release the big end caps on the A2, A3 and A5 cylinders from both A and B sides. These are marked with all the datum marks and placed aside. Now we can have our lunch!

After a well-earned 20-minute break, including watching the trains call at Churston station, we set to again. The crane is employed to lift out the three cylinders and con-rods, after barring the engine round to the correct position each time. Hopefully the cylinder liners will draw out easily because of the damaged seals. This stage was completed just before the crane operator had to clock off for the day. Us Laira lads carried on, though, cleaning up the block and cylinder liners. Lastly I take out all the defective seals so that we can make a clean start on the reassembly next morning. The tools are put away and the roof hatches on the loco secured, and then at 7pm it's time to go home. There have not been any major hiccups but the day has just vanished, and there is plenty more hard graft in store tomorrow. We are very weary and have oil-stained hair and arms, which will take some shifting. A salient reminder that sentiment alone is not enough to keep a Class 50 running.

Muscles aching we book on again at 0630, wondering if the refitting can be squeezed into a single day, as it is necessarily a more delicate task than the removal. Churston is reached in heavy drizzle - that's all we need! We clamber over the damp loco and open the roof hatches, then give the cylinder liners a final clean and fit new O rings on the cylinders.

The crane swings into action to press the liners into position. I can now check the pistons, rings, and big end shells before spacing each piston ring for replacement. Now the crane gently pops the first piston into the cylinder, we bolt up the big end and

repin, and then repeat the operation twice more. Again there have not been any hitches but it is a time consuming job. We are both starting to flag, yet have to press on before the craneman knocks off at 1630. A late lunch is taken, just 15 minutes break today, then the reserves of strength are summoned up to screw in those cylinder head nuts. It's only now that most of the fifties have been withdrawn that we come to appreciate how much the beasts took out of us! At least the rain has stopped, though it is unpleasantly humid. Applying 600Ibs of torque to the nuts requires not just brute force but a good foothold and balance too.

Time is slipping by, and the awkward bits are still to fit, but at least the cranework has been completed in time. The workshop staff leave for home and tea, but we have to tussle with the A2 exhaust manifold flange, which will not line up. A mighty heave and struggle and the thing at last behaves. The exhaust manifold inlets and coolant heatshields are now refitted, then the push rod rockers and fuel pipes etc. are put back. The tappets are adjusted, though we will have to leave the final coolant test and oil change to the Devon Diesel Group. 8.30pm, the roof hatches are shut and we are done (and done in!). Drained of energy and aching all over we crawl off home: no problem in getting to sleep tonight! On the plus side, there has been plenty of job satisfaction, and it is a 'first' for Laira to work on a private line. 'Superb' duly reenters traffic and wows the crowds on the picturesque Paignton — Kingswear line.

3: The East Lancashire Railway

At home one evening the phone rings: it's a long — lost friend from Lancashire, whom I haven't seen since Hydraulic days. We swap stories and then he asks "What's the state of 'Thunderer' and 'Valiant' now that they are officially withdrawn'?" Well, I reply, both are still in working order, but bear in mind that neither has seen a major overhaul since refurbishment at Doncaster; December 1981 in the case of 50008 and February 1981 for 50015. How come, I ask, do you know someone who might be interested in buying them'?

Could be, is the reply, and so I suggest that he rings Laira to fix up a meeting with the Area Fleet Manager.

I am intrigued, as at this stage I have no idea who the mystery purchaser might be, though the home for the locos would be the East Lancs Railway. A few days later a mate at work tells me that Pete Waterman is to visit the depot. Pete Who'? Never heard of him! It is gently explained to me that he is a famous record producer, and even has a TV show. Not surprisingly, the visit generates some excitement. I am summoned to the Manager's office to be told that '08 and '15 are to be stabled outside

No.6 road tomorrow in order to be run up for inspection by a potential private purchaser. September 9th 1992 is the day, and after our meal break I meet my Lancashire pal and am introduced to the pop guru. It turns out he is an ex-BR fireman and a very down—to-earth sort. After going to the main office we make our way outside to the locos. Both visitors express surprise at the good external condition of the fifties. Finger on the start button and both locos are started up; they are given a thorough examination of bogies, engines and state of the bodywork. I also carry out a brake, power and DSD test from each cab. To cut a long story short, the decision is made to go all out for a purchase bid. Back go PW and my friend to the Manager's Office to start the negotiations.

Hopefully this will gel and '08 and '15 could then enter preservation together, just as they had ended their days with BR together.

The sale tender produced a lot of interest, with 15 parties bidding for the locos, but it was PW who came out on top to become the proud owner of 'Thunderer' and co-owner of 'Valiant'. So it was that on September 22nd the celebrity 'Hitman' returned to Laira to officially take over the ownership of '08 and have a 'Thundering' good time. He danced when piped onto the footplate by the Captain of the Royal Naval College in Plymouth that shared the 'Thunderer' name, and was presented with the ship's crest while the loco received a rousing musical send off from the naval band. Then the man behind pop stars such as Bananarama and Kylie Minogue told the assembled throng that the fifties were to live at Bury, in the same county as their birthplace in 1968.

Clearance to move the pair by rail to Longsight depot in Manchester was granted, and three days later 47377 arrives to tow them away from their long-time Devon home. I make the statutory brake test before the special working can leave, and wonder when I will see my favourite 50008 again. The important thing, though, is that both '08 and '15 have been saved!

Another phone call at home: it is PW, inviting me to come up to the East Lancs as one of his guests for the reintroduction to traffic of the pair at the Diesel Gala at the start of October. This is only days away, but of course the answer is yes.

It is at least ten years since I last set foot on Bury Bolton Street station, when ex—Laira Hydraulics D832 'Onslaught' and D1041 'Western Prince` arrived. Then the line up to Rawtenstall was still in BR hands and due for closure, seeing Class 40s on the last few scrap iron trains. Now it is busy with preservation traffic, and further reopening is on the cards. The trip up from Devon with my eldest son is a slow one: traffic nose to tail on a rain swept M62. We take a lunch break at Bescot (viewing the depot in the shadow of the M5/M6 interchange), and on the motorway see 'Battle of Britain' steamer 34072 heading south on a low-loader, returning from loan to the East Lancs. In the boot are Class 50 line drawings of the mechanical and electrical systems, fault finding guides, tools and the inevitable hand lamp.

Finally, at 4pm we drive into the old Midland Railway Yard at Bury, and find my friend busy giving shunting orders to his green-liveried Class 24; D5054.

50008 is standing in Platform 3, and its new owner tells us that alas all is not well. Upon arrival from Longsight it was found that 'Thunderer' was suffering repeated engine shutdowns. However, a volunteer on the East Lancs had discovered that a resistor had burnt through on the KV10 board, and was in the town at that very moment buying a replacement. Meanwhile, 'Valiant' was still at Longsight (which it probably had not visited since freightliner duties in the late 1960s), but was due to be moved by low loader across Manchester tonight. The crucial resistor is bought from an ordinary electrical store - price 50p — and we duly solder it in place. '08 is started up, and gradually notched up to test that all engine speeds are now OK. By this time PW was away to a gig until the early hours, but we gave the fifty its first outing in preservation in the form of a test run to Summerseat and back. Unfortunately, the screw coupling was hanging too low and caught the wooden barrow crossing there; but without causing any damage, thank goodness. Apart from that '08 is running smoothly, and so back at Bury we settle down in the railway cabin to a most welcome fish and chip supper.

That evening I meet three BR lads from Longsight depot, who would help maintain the fifties on the East Lancs. After a final check over '08, so as to be ready for the morning, we all adjourn to the local, beside the railway yard entrance, for a jar or two. At about 11.30pm what should we see through the window but a Fifty — there was definitely no getting away from them! 'Valiant' on its low loader had arrived, and was backed into the yard to be unloaded in daylight.

Next morning my son and I drive down from the hotel and find '08 in the process of being reunited with its crests. Blue 03073 is already giving rides out to Buckley Wells shed with an ex—Bury line EMU, still in its orange and brown colours. The diagram for 'Thunderer' is the 1030 departure to Rawtenstall and back, and then a rededication ceremony with 'Valiant' at 1430, at which naval personnel from Plymouth will be present.

'08 is started. up and waits to become a passenger loco again. The Hymek, though, is pushed back into the shed having failed with flat batteries. D5054 is used to winch '15 off the low loader. PW climbs on board ready for the first public run, despite only having had four hours' sleep and with another gig ahead of him tonight. We power up to the signal and soon set back onto the stock in Platform 3. The whistle is blown and with a triumphant toot on the horn 'Thunderer' begins a new chapter in its life.

I am delighted to be part of the event, and feel quite at home with all the erstwhile Laira locos around - a Warship, a Western, and now a pair of fifties. At Ramsbottom, the halfway point on the line, we are held to await a crossing train, and a Longsight fitter and I have a look round the engine room; nothing to report. Despite not having been parted from '15 for many months, '08 is working well. Rawtenstall station is entered at 15mph, and we glide to a halt at the buffer stops. Most of the station buildings have been rebuilt with local sandstone in Midland Railway style, and what with the upper quadrant semaphores, it is a grand sight. We detach and run round, and are off back down the line in quarter of an hour.

Through the flicking of the windscreen wipers (the rain having set in) we see as we enter Bury that '15 is firmly back on the rails. 'Valiant' is stabled in Castlecroft Goods Yard, home of the former Bury Transport Museum.

After a quick lunch we examine '15, and find trouble on trying to start the fifty: its batteries have gone flat. The Longsight lads come over to assist,

having commandeered a battery charger. With the loco on charge we complete the rest of the examination, anxiously wondering whether '15 will be right in time for the 2.30pm ceremony. Crowds of fans are watching from the embankment and overbridge; even the local police are in evidence. After half an hour on charge we discuss the plan of action: one of us will hit the start button, one will monitor the engine governor, and one the engine lubricating oil pump. On the shout "Go for it!!" 'Valiant' is kick-started into life, showering soot and exhaust over everyone. Back in the electrical cubicle the charge rate is monitored as the charger is disconnected, and the engine left on idle to reduce the hunting and clouds of exhaust that are wafting across the yard. My throat is very dry, and a kind gentleman sends me over a cuppa from the cabin. Brake and power tests are made, and then '08 rumbles out of Bolton Street Tunnel and sets back onto the stock in Platform 3. '15 is to be attached to the front for the run up to Ramsbottom, where it will be taken off. As such, the locos are connected in tandem and not in multiple. By now 'Valiant's' engine temperature is up to normal, but it is still smoky and, of course, has not been powered up since leaving Laira. '15 is fouling the wooden crossing and '08 is too far from the microphone, and so arrangements are made to wave the fifties back into the platform. They are then shut down and

50015 'Valiant' and 50008 'Thunderer' and their initial start up at the East Lancashire Railway - October 1992. Photo: Mike Woodhouse

Pete Waterman and the delegation of sailors and officers from the Navy perform the cresting ceremony on 'Thunderer'.

About twenty minutes late the formalities are over, and the twins are restarted for the first ever doubleheaded Class 50 run in preservation. Despite the rain they make a glorious spectacle, and many admirers have braved the weather to savour the sight. All goes well on the trip to Ramsbottom, where '15 comes off and retires to the goods loop. '08 continues solo to Rawtenstall` (a weight restriction on a bridge prevents further doubleheading), and 'Valiant' makes good the time until its pal returns by shunting a demonstration freight train around the station.

A pairing of a Class 40 and a Class 52 arrive to cross the return Class 50 working. '15 is hitched up again and the celebrity locos return to Bury. It is time for PW to go and record another TV show, no doubt to earn the pennies needed to keep his new charges thundering on.

Update: Pete Waterman eventually sold his Fifties: 50015 is still on the ELR and ably looked after by the Bury Valiant Group. 50008 had a more chequered life, but is now secure, being operated on the mainline by Hanson and Hall.

4: The Bodmin and Wenford Railway

This story of 50042 'Triumph' starts one morning on No.3 road at Laira depot. A timeworn '42 has been sent back from Exeter with a bad exhaust blow, and it is my task to investigate the problem. I start the loco's engine and enter the hot engine room to carry out a full examination, soon discovering that the B1 exhaust bellows is split and needs to be replaced. After discussion with the supervisor it is decided to remove it while still hot, and let it then cool down as we have a tea break. With sweat dripping of our brows and arms black with soot we succeed in removing the offending item.

After the break new parts are obtained from the stores, and the refit is made. By the time the engine has been run up and tested word has come through that '42 will also have an 'A' exam and brake adjustment. This does not take long, and soon 'Triumph' is back in action in the Engineers' DCWA pool. However, the end was nigh. The final working came a week or so later, on October 14th 1990, when after hauling trains for the Civil Engineer in the Exeter area it returned to Laira for withdrawal. Once the last rites of removing the nameplates had been done (these being placed in the Stores before going to Collector's Corner at Euston), '42 joined its fellows in Ocean Siding and later Tavistock Junction, there to languish quietly awaiting its fate: either a preservationist buyer or the cutter's torch.

A year on, and 'Triumph' is one of the lucky ones, having been purchased by a diesel group based on the Bodmin and Wenford Railway. So, a fifty will be saved in Cornwall.

Alas, the thieves have taken their toll, with all the main cabling cut through and removed throughout the engine room, and most of the windows smashed. On the morning of December 8rd 1991 the local Class 08 Transfer trip sees 50020/026/036/040/042/043/045 dragged back to the depot, all bar 'Triumph' and 'Eagle' destined for the scrap merchant.

Instructions were given to replace the windows in '42 with those from other withdrawn fifties, and also the main cabling from the doomed 50010. Our own group with 50049 and the Bodmin people with 50042 worked side by side at this time, as 'Triumph' was prepared for the move into Cornwall and preservation status.

Once the Bodmin base had been reached, in March 1992, a full survey was carried out, one of the first jobs being to replace the broken windows and make the cabs secure. The next aim was to get the engine running as soon as possible, though an awful lot of work was required as two years of being stored in the open had allowed water ingress and all the troubles stemming from that. The engine itself along with two turbochargers were seized solid, and there was a considerable amount of water in several of the cylinders. All the decompressors were removed and the water sucked out, this being replaced by a mixture of diesel fuel oil and engine oil. While this was in progress the main traction power cables were replaced. At long last the battery was charged and the engine barred over until free of coolant: the loco could now be started!

It is now the summer of 1992, and I receive a phone call at home to say that the big day will be August 13th. Summer or not, it is pouring with rain as we drive off down the A38, and the further west we go, the wetter is gets. By mid afternoon l arrive at Bodmin General station, where the diesel group welcomes me. There is '42, still in its washed—out large logo livery, but much restored inside. Fuel, oil and coolant are checked, the decompressors are secured, and then the magic start button is pressed. The engine turns and coughs reluctantly into life, throwing water, rust, soot and oil out through the four exhaust stacks. We cheer, and not even the weather can dampen our sense of triumph: another fifty has made it back into life. After all this excitement we have a bite to eat and a celebration drink at the railway hostelry over the road.

This power unit only did three months work after Crewe overhaul, and so should see good service for the Bodmin and Wenford Railway. Of course, there was a lot more hard work and sheer dedication before the loco could haul passengers again, but in

September 1993 50042 was back in revenue earning service for the first time in three years.

Project Defiance

The fifties first intruded into my private life towards the end of 1981, when I attended the inaugural meeting of the Class 50 Locomotive Group, held in the Great Western Hotel at Paddington. Little did l realise that a decade later, as the Class 50 Society, we would be the proud owners of what was destined to be the Railfreight prototype, 50149. A lot of miles have passed under the bridge in that time, and the sales of both Blood, Sweat and Fifties and Thundering Fifties have made a small contribution to keeping 'Defiance' on the rails.

Let's now look at the loco and how we came to buy and restore it. 449 was a bit special from the start, as not only was it the final Class 50, but also it was last ever mixed traffic diesel — electric locomotive built for British Rail. Not only that, it was the last such loco for BR to come out of the famous Vulcan Foundry in Lancashire. Costing a mere £127,000, it was delivered in Rail Blue new to Crewe Diesel depot on December 11th 1968. Work on WCML expresses to Glasgow along with some freightliner duties followed, until transfer to the Bristol Bath Road on the Western Region in May 1974. Renumbering from 449 to 50049 had taken place at the start of that year. Duties were mainly expresses on what is now known as the GWML, though with emphasis switching from Bristol to the West

Country after the arrival of the HST fleet in 1975. As a result the loco moved to Laira in April 1977, and parcels, milk and the occasional clay train were added to the repertoire.

May 2nd 1978 was a special day for '49, for it was then that I fitted the 'Defiance' nameplates. For a while it had the privilege of carrying the power unit from the Class 50 prototype DP2, and was a notably good runner at the time. By contrast, the loco was a real headache in the latter part of 1982, when it suffered long periods out of action due to persistent fuel starvation problems. These were infuriatingly difficult to cure, and we even resorted to cutting open the main fuel tank, the scar of which can still be seen today. In the end '49 was sent to Doncaster for refurbishing, in the new year of 1983.

'Defiance' emerged in the then-standard 'large logo' livery, which was embellished with a black roof and red buffer beams after repainting during an 'E' exam in 1986. Then came the 'F' exam programme, and the decision to have '49 as the trial loco for Railfreight use (See Page 22). Thus it became the only Class 50 to carry the three-tone grey Railfreight livery in BR ownership, with red-and-yellow Distribution sub-sector decals.

Even the nameplates were repainted, having black letters on a yellow background. On its maiden trip it nearly stalled going up Hemerdon, and then became derailed at Exeter Riverside, sustaining relatively minor traction motor flashover damage. No sooner was this sorted out then it wrecked its engine ten days before the official adhesion trials

50042 'Triumph' has been resident on the Bodmin and Wenford Railway since purchase from British Rail. Seen here in at Bodmin General on a driving experience train. Photo: Craig Munday

for Railfreight were due. These were scheduled to take place between Westbury and Warminster on Sunday October 18th 1988, with varying loads and rail conditions. The aim was to see if the regeared Class 50 had the haulage capacity of a pair of Class 33s, and so could take over ballast workings to the Southern Region from Meldon Quarry.

Laira had to work round the clock to get a new engine in and calibrated for this high-profile event. So, on October 8th 50014 was working Waterloo 'Network Expresses'; and on the 9th it had surrendered it's power until, never to work again! (Sorry Andy!) 'Defiance', though, was repaired in time to undertake the trials. Although fairly successful, the lack of sanding gear, removed during the 1980s refurbishment, was an Achilles heel, and the vision of a fleet of 50/1s never materialised.

Instead 50149 was a one-off oddity, confined to Departmental duties in the South West. Rarely did it get to haul passengers, though on January 2nd 1988 it was called on to assist the 1344 Penzance — Paddington from Par to Exeter. HST power cars 43034/141 were deficient only thanks to a speedo defect, and so the run over the South Devon banks from Plymouth to Exeter was completed in a spirited 54 minutes - including a stop at Totnes! From April 1988 '149 entered the FTLL pool, where it was used alongside Class 37/5s to take china clay from the various dries in Cornwall to Fowey Docks. Places such as Burngullow, Drinnick Mill and Parkandillack became regular haunts. Effectively 'Defiance' was covering for 37670/671, which had sustained severe collision damage at Tavistock Junction Yard in November 1987, and when they returned to traffic early in 1989 the one-off fifty was consigned to general Departmental duties in the DCWA pool, working off Bristol East Depot and Exeter Riverside. This only lasted for some four weeks, and then the loco was stopped at Laira for re—conversion to a standard 100mph Class 50. A double bogie swap, courtesy of 50040, and repaint into NSE colours was complete by March 17th 1989. The scene was set for the last year and a quarter of '49's active service, turn and turn about with the rest of the NSSA Fifties on the Exeter-Waterloo route. Then, on 1st August 1991, it hauled the 0840 from Waterloo and on arrival at Exeter was sent light to Laira, never to work again. Withdrawal came on the 16th, for no other reason than that the cost of a 'D' exam and rectifying an engine governor fault were not sanctioned. Off came the nameplates, and '49 joined its dead colleagues in the Lipson sidings. Meanwhile, back in September 1990 the Class 50 Society-had launched its share appeal in an attempt to raise enough funds to buy a Fifty in a year or so's time. It seemed a tall order, with bids expected at anything up to £25,000 per

loco. No particular machine was held in mind, instead the choice would be dictated by whichever one was in best condition when offered for sale. In May 1991 tenders were issued for 50019/035/036, but it seemed better to wait until after the fallout from the expected major cutback in the NSE fleet in October. This proved to be a wise move, as several locos were then offered in almost ready—to-run condition. Our bid (of £7,000) was sufficient to make us the proud owners of 50049, the decision being announced on December 16th. Not only had we succeeded in saving a Class 50, but we had landed the unique Railfreight experimental loco! Unsurprisingly, the Society voted to return the loco to its 50149 guise.

An agreement was reached with the AFM to keep 'Defiance' at Laira while restoration took place, with the volunteers working to strict safety rules. The first working party took place on January 25th 1992, to assess the work that needed to be done. For me this was the start of many hours of my spare time working on the loco - often straight after clocking off from being paid for working on other locos! Through the winter the engine was barred over occasionally, to keep it free running and clear of rainwater. All the wheelsizes were taken and recorded, with the bogies being found to be in generally very good condition.

Spring saw the real work start, notably the cleaning of the main generator to prevent the dreaded flashover problem. Chris Holland and Richard Holmes, on the staff at Bristol Bath Road and members of the Society from the start, emerged from their inspection of the genny unrecognisable in a thick coat of oily, black gunge. My main job was the refurbishment of No.1 cab, so that it could shown off to visitors.

May 9th was a red-letter day. For the first time '49 was started up in preservation, in fact the first time for the loco in nearly two years. This was after carefully pumping the sump oil around the engine and checking all the bearings and rockers. With scarcely a splutter 'Defiance' roared into life again, soon ticking over sweetly and showing no signs of needing attention. However, the B1 cylinder was rather weak, and consequently more smoky than the others. It was a really heartening sight, to see our loco alive once more: so much had been achieved in a relatively short time, thanks to the dedication of our band of volunteers.

A private limited company — Project Defiance — was formed at this time, to protect the shareholder owners of the loco. Negotiations were entered into with Railfreight Distribution at Manchester to sponsor a repaint into the striking triple-grey livery. Replica nameplates and 'Laira Galleon' cabside plaques were ordered in readiness for the repaint. Then came a body blow: Railfreight had to drop out of the deal, leaving us to arrange and fund the painting ourselves. On the positive side, though, HMS Defiance (part of the Devonport naval base) offered to supply us with replica crests, as worn by '149 in its Railfreight days.

By the end of the summer No.1 cab was resplendent with reupholstered cab seats, carpets, chromed fitments and having had a thorough internal repaint. Meanwhile, the cleaning and repairing of all movable parts - both mechanical and cosmetic - continued.

Attention then turned to the electronic equipment. This continued into 1993, a year greeted with great excitement as it should see the public relaunch of our 'Defiance'.

When the weather improved we set about rubbing down the bodyside, to provide a smooth, sound surface for the new livery. Off came the NSE decals, then the sanding discs were put to work.

Underneath the NSE paintwork we found the original Railfreight decals, and so were able to get their precise measurements and positions. The few dents, scratches and rust spots were dealt with at this stage, though '49 was in better condition in this respect than most other fifties. Elsewhere, the roof panels required re—riveting, and the cab door and window seals renewing. Four injectors had been reconditioned and recalibrated for the B1 to B4 cylinders. The dedication and cheerfulness - plus fish and chips — kept our band of merry men working on, and steady progress was made.

Soon we were ready for the repainting. A check with the stores revealed that all the paint colours had arrived, but to my horror the transfer decals were too small, being the same as those used on Class 86s. After looking through the catalogue we discovered that the sizing for 50149 was a one-off, and so we decided to paint them using the measurements of the old ones. This should last longer, as the transfers tended to fade over the years and the edges would start to lift. Down came our professional bodywork painters, and over a period of six Saturdays 50049 was transformed into a gleaming 50149. August 18th was announced as the day when the

rededication and recresting would take place - two full years after withdrawal. With a date to work to, even more effort was put in, with extra special attention being given to the detail of the paintwork. On went the yellow nameplates and the crests and plaques. Working parties continued inside the loco too, with the B1 injector being replaced in early August. By the 14th '149 was berthed on No.1 road at Laira, looking absolutely immaculate and awaiting the BR inspection on the following day. I was on nights that week, but of course did not want to miss the final preparations. As dusk fell on the 17th we washed and then polished the loco, until it looked better than new. Next morning, the Captain of HMS Defiance arrived to rededicate 50149 in an official ceremony, with the AFM and railway press in attendance.

It was a great day, and I felt very proud. 'Defiance' had been saved, and would shortly move to its new home at Allied Steel & Wire in Cardiff, as well as putting in a starring appearance at the forthcoming Newport and Worksop Open Days.

Update: Project Defiance and The Fifty Fund operated together for several years both on the mainline and preserved railways before agreeing to merge.

This was completed in 2006 and bought together both an unrivalled set of spare parts and expertise in the mechanical, electrical, electronic aspects of these complex locomotives. The organisation also benefits from a management team that includes financial, business, sales and railway operations experience.

Currently the Alliance has it's six locomotives based on the Severn Valley Railway and access to the excellent dedicated diesel maintenance facilities on site at Kidderminster.

50049 and 50007 in the striking GBRF livery on the 50 Terminator Phoenixed Railtour - 23rd March 2019. Photo: Ian Walken

Glorious Fifties

Introduction

It is 2010 and I am sitting on a bench seat at Marsh Mills station on the Plym Valley Railway. My three young grandsons are with me, Joseph, Kieran and Hayden. I am sharing my Werthers Original toffees as Grandads do.

50017 'Royal Oak' is beside us, its English Electric 16 cylinder CSVT engine at idling, with exhaust light blue haze.

I am asked if there are anymore stories from the shop floor about Class 50s. I had absolutely no idea at the amount of interest there would be in my first and second books, Blood Sweat and Fifties and Thundering Fifties, which were tales of the Class 50s from the workshop floor. By now, some sixteen years later, the only copies of these books are available on eBay!

It is my privilege to present the final part in this trilogy — 'Glorious Fifties' . To start with, I will go back fifty years and then end up in preservation. The following pages are a tribute to all the work forces that keep Class 50s running on the tracks of the United Kingdom — well done to all.

Happy reading!!!

Mike Woodhouse
Ivybridge, Devon -2010

With special thanks to:
My dear wife Val, my children and grandchildren, my dear friends Geoff Hudson and Dicky Daw; Class 50 colleagues, Paul Furtek and the Project Defiance team.

Preface

It is now eighteen years since Class 50s were in revenue earning service and sixteen years since the last Class 50 saw service with British Rail.

Mike Woodhouse has long been associated with the diesel locomotive era, and even in retirement, turns his hand to help out and also provides invaluable advice to those struggling with these temperamental machines. In his third book of the series Mike not only relates some memories of the early years, but also concentrates on the period between 1992 and 1994 when the three remaining Class 50s were kept for charter work.

Such was the following with the Class 50s that I was determined to see them out in style and at the same time give the public as much access as was reasonably practical.

The 'Girls' — as they became known at Laira — performed numerous rail tours in a variety of liveries and performed faultlessly for their public. · All this could not have been achieved without the dedication of the staff at Laira who not only kept the 'Girls' going but frequently went the extra mile.

So how did they do it? Perhaps Mike will let you know! Geoff Hudson
Area Fleet Manager, Plymouth, 1989- 1996

School Boy's Surprise - Summer 1958

My first story of -'Glorious Fifties' is about my very first encounter with the English Electric 16 cylinder SVT engine. Some 50 years ago as a teenage schoolboy living in Greenford in Middlesex near the Grand Union Canal, Sunday afternoon trips to the locomotive sheds of the WR and LMR were the order of the day. My mate Chris and I would cycle the tow path from Greenford to Acton as this was a safe and quick way to 81A Old Oak Common and IA Willesden locomotive sheds which stood along each bank in West London. Armed with duffle bag, notebook, pen, jam sandwiches, a Lyons individual fruit pie and a bottle of Tizer, we would weave our way past Sunday walkers and various people fishing from the canal bank.

On reaching 81A Old Oak Common shed we would chain our bicycles to the iron fence railings, near to the railwayman's allotments. We then bunked around the four turntable roundhouse and the workshop, known as the 'Factory', which was always exciting to see. I had no idea at this time that I would later be working in this place, in fact in about two years' time, as a Workshop Craft Engineer apprentice.

81A on this Sunday afternoon was stacked out with numerous locos of the Western Region, plus the early type English Electric shunting locomotives, which later became re-numbered as Class 08s. We got around without meeting the dreaded locomotive Shed Foreman, thus getting all the locomotive numbers that were on shed into our notebooks. On returning to the allotments, we sat on the canal bank and consumed our jam sandwiches and drank our Tizer.

We then un-chained our bicycles before crossing the canal bridge on Old Oak Common Lane en-route to 1A Willesden depot. I remember seeing London Transport Trolley buses on the 660 route. Turning left into Stephenson Street the terraced houses backed onto 1A's roundhouse. Once again we chained up our bicycles near the storage road beside the roundhouse and made our way in. This roundhouse was tidied up for the exhibition in 1951 for a public display of new British Railway steam and diesel locomotives.

What a view it was on this particular Sunday as the whole turntable roads were full of diesels. 10000/01 BR green, 10201/02/03, BR green and the first D5XXX, (later Class 24s), new English Electric D8XXX (later Class 20) all in new Brunswick green livery, a few grubby 08 shunting locomotives, with not a yellow nose panel in sight. After walking round we came across a mechanical engineer who was draining out oil from 10201. We started speaking to him with enthusiasm about diesels in general. As it was a quiet Sunday afternoon he asked if we would like to walk through 10201 to see the engine room layout and we duly accepted. For the first time in my life I saw an English Electric I6 cylinder SVT power unit, its huge size towering above us. Asking how engineers repaired it the answer came back — "with difficulty". We walked through 10201 to the other cab and climbed down. The visit was brief and we then thanked the engineer as we made our way to the workshop and the old steam shed on the bank of the canal. Again, 1A Willesden was packed with all types of London Midland Region steam locomotives. Again, after adding all the numbers on shed to our notebooks we returned to our bicycles and made our way back home along the canal to tell Mum and Dad of our Sunday afternoon trip. 50 years has now elapsed and that engineer was right about the English Electric power units being

The loco that inspired a career: Bulleid designed 1750HP Diesel Electric10201 outside Willesden shed in the company of 10001 on 17th April 55 . Photo: Ranwell Collection—Rail Photoprints

repaired 'with difficulty', as I later found out working on the Class 50s. Now it is over to the preservation groups to do the same.

50019 Off the Road: A Diary of Events

This story is one of the hardest Class 50 events of my life while working on British Rail and one

The twins (10000 and 10001) burst out of Preston Brook Tunnel in 1958 with the head up the Royal Scot. Photo: R.A. Whitfield—Rail Photoprints

which comes straight from the heart. I am a third of the way through my railway career when out of the blue I am hit by a bombshell — 50019 to be precise. It is 1976 and a heavy winter was followed by a long hot summer, both of them record breakers. 50019s derailment at Reading on Wednesday 2nd June, struck me very hard. The events of that week began on a Sunday — Friday 06.30—14.30 early shift, working on Laira-allocated locomotives, Classes 08, 25, 46, 47, 50 and 52. Although the reign of the Class 52 'Western' diesel hydraulics was nearing an end, twenty five were still in service at this time. Diesel electric types, including Class 50s, were also under maintenance in the workshop.

Tuesday 1st June — just an ordinary working day. At 06.30, my mate and I were given the worksheets of a `B` exam to be varied out on 50019 by our supervisor. The loco was in BR blue livery, un-named and un-refurbished, and was berthed in number five road at Laira depot awaiting servicing. After getting our tools, lamps, gauges and filters together, we set about our daily task with myself taking the locomotives underframe, beneath the sole bar. This inspection was an end-to-end of all the fixtures and fittings, bogies, sizes of tyres, wheels, frames, pipes, compressors, fuel tanks and air reservoirs. Once the shift was nearing the end we both wrote up our daily worksheets, including other repairs to be carried out before 50019 could re-enter traffic.

As a pattern, my shift `B` would be followed by `C` at 14.30—22.30, but, for reasons unknown, 50019 lay untouched for eight hours until the night gang, `A` shift, commenced at 22.30-06.30. This gang took on the outstanding repairs, engine run-up and release sheet. By early morning 2nd June, 50019 was ready to re-enter traffic, to which it was allocated 1A45, the 12.20 Penzance—Paddington from Plymouth North Road station.

My own duties on that Wednesday were working in the Laira workshop on the early shift.

At home that evening whilst having a family evening meal with the television on for the 18.00 evening news, breaking news was brought to my attention about a serious derailment at Reading station. My heart missed several beats when I saw it was 50019, GUV S86736, W14074 and W5452. Devastated by what I had witnessed on the television, a sleepless night lay ahead of the unfolding events.

Thursday 3rd June at 06.30 I book on duty at Laira and I am asked to go upstairs to the Area Fleet Managers office. The `A` shift night men, `B` shift Supervisor, my mate and I all attend. We all knew the circumstances. Our A.F.M explained that 50019 had left the road at the approach to Reading station. Fortunately there had been no injuries and the train was evacuated with the passengers being escorted along the track to Reading station, from where they continued their journeys by other services.

50019, the track, signals and cables were all severely damaged and the disruption to the railway was considerable. The A.F.M outlined that a Board of Trade inquiry would be held the next day — Friday 4th June - at the Western Tower headquarters at Reading station from 10.00.

All six Laira personnel plus the A.F.M and two trade union representatives would be required to travel to Reading to face judge and jury, headed by Major Peter Olver.

Friday 4th June at 07.00, we travelled on the Plymouth—Paddington 'Golden Hind' service, hauled by a Class 50 with Mark II air-conditioned coaches in blue grey livery. The mood was somber with light conversation, newspapers, coffee and nervous talk of the day ahead that we all faced. On the approach to Reading station we could see the aftermath of the derailment - a sight which truly shocked me.

The enquiry was very daunting as each member faced questions of 50019's workload on Tuesday 1st June. My throat kept going dry as I answered the questions put to me about 50019's wheel sets and bogies.

I felt very alone, at a total loss at this point, but answered with honesty and integrity all the questions put by Major Peter Olver. I knew I had given 50019's bogies a 110% examination, so what went dramatically wrong on that journey up to Paddington? At this stage I was at a complete loss to know. One minute I had been doing an everyday routine job and the next I was standing in the dock being questioned over an incident which had made the national headlines.

Part of the Gibson Ring, which held the steel tyre to the wheel, had been found at Fairwood junction, west of Westbury, and yet 50019 travelled some seventy to eighty miles at high speeds before derailing as it slowed on the approach to Reading station on a very sharp twenty mile an hour curve. The history of the wheel set with 50019 which failed at Reading was as follows:

Built by Taylor Brothers in 1968 and fitted new to locomotive D417: (50017). In 1971, D417 travelled 267,580 miles before being retyred at Crewe works. This wheelset was then placed under 50016, which in traffic travelled a further 152,270 miles before having new tyres fitted.

In 1973 Crewe works placed the wheel set under 50019 which then travelled a further 240,000 miles before the failure occurred. 50019's service history from its delivery to British Rail London Midland Region had run a total of 791,250 miles in service. This was a total of 243,750 miles since its last works overhaul. On the Western Region of British Rail approximately 202,500 were covered.

For safety reasons, all Class 50s that night of 2nd June had a wheel and tyre check for loose Gibson Rings, although none were recorded. After being re—railed by the Old Oak Common breakdown unit, 50019 was removed to Reading diesel depot yard. A spare bogie was sought from Crewe works and sent to Reading where 50019 was rebogied. The loco was then towed to Crewe works for underframe collision repairs.

After the inquiry concluded an unknown reason as to why its number one left hand wheel set had failed (the tyre parting from the wheel set), myself and other Laira colleagues breathed a sigh of relief at such a traumatic experience. It was the lowest point of my railway career and thankfully one that was never to be repeated!

Some fourteen years later 50019 was saved from the Grim Reaper and twenty years later is residing in preservation on the Mid Norfolk Railway.

Fury With 'Furious': 50034 at Old Oak Common 1979

During this period the Class 50s were suffering heavy casualties with main generator failures (the Achilles heel of the Class) with power earth faults. At Old Oak Common 50034 'Furious' in standard British Rail blue livery was one of them. Due to heavy work commitments at B.R.E.L's Doncaster works, it was decided to tow 50034 to Laira for a power unit lift and to change the main generator. At this time it was necessary to lift the power unit outside in the open, by using the Ransom Rapier forty five tonne steam crane. Power unit lifts were the biggest heavy jobs undertaken on the Class 50, especially on a depot basis, as this was usually a major works operation. Planning and man power had to be slotted into Laira`s day-to—day maintenance program. A main generator was ordered from Doncaster works, while 50034 was to be towed west to Laira depot.

On arrival, the Old Oak Common locomotive was very dirty and it was found to have parts missing as the locomotive had been heavily cannibalized to keep other class 50 locomotives in service.

Berthed in number five road work started to get under way with the removal of all the roof sections, exhaust stacks, etc.

This was then followed by lifting out the electric train heat/auxiliary generator. Shifts of `A`, `B` and `C` gangs worked round the clock to disconnect the English Electric power unit in 50034 ready for the big lift. 50034 was then towed outside the main workshop onto the concrete area beside the steam crane, which was ideal for packing and stabilizing the jacks.

The early morning shift from 06.30—14.30 would carry out the lift as apprentices could be on hand to look out for any snags during the lift out. The forty

five tonne steam crane was lit up by the night operator, thus making steam for the early turn crane driver when he arrived on duty.

Lift day arrived and myself, two other litters, plus the allotted apprentices from `B` shift started the task of the power unit removal. Desmond, our crane driver, swung the jib with the heavy lifting beam so that it could be coupled up to the power unit. On the orders of our supervisor the jib slowly lifted the power unit skywards. This delicate maneuver took place over a three hour period, after which the power unit was gently lowered onto a rectank wagon fitted with Class 50 beams. The wagon was then shunted into number live or six road for the change over of the main generator. Another day dawned on the early shift for another lift - this time in reverse order to refit the replacement power unit. However, this time it had to be with a lot more precision as the power unit has to correctly align with the bed plates on the locomotive's engine room floor. This is a time consuming task which was completed some seven hours later.

The shift over, 50034 was shunted back into the main shed's number five road for its replacement components to be fitted. Meanwhile Old Oak Common had sent all the parts removed from the loco before departure to Laira to make 50034 complete once again.

Over the next couple of days 50034 was brought back to working life. Everybody worked well and hard to achieve this as it was the first ever power unit lift at depot level on the Western Region. 50034's power unit systems were primed, the start button was pressed and the engine burst into life .... but not for long. The Class 50 was then shunted outside because of the exhaust fumes in the main workshop. 50034 was then berthed outside in number four road on the fuelling point after a hard weeks work on the main generator exchange as it was ready for a light engine trial run to Totnes and return. Laira always had a Monday to Friday trial run crew for such occasions. The crew for the trip comprised a fitter, an apprentice and an electrician together with the locomotive's driver. As we took power to proceed out to the Laira shed dummy signal in readiness for the trial run to Totnes, the power earth fault lamp illuminated, accompanied by a total loss of power. Reset, and try again but the power earth fault tripped once more. Thus 50034 is a complete failure!

I walked back to the supervisor's office to relay the news. The depots Class 08 diesel electric shunter was summoned to drag us back into number four road. An investigation began with just about all grades from top management down as to why the newly fitted main generator had an earth fault. All the carbon brushes were removed and the

In May 1979 an unrefurbished 50034 has its power unit swapped at Plymouth's Laira Depot after a main generator failure. Photo: Mike Woodhouse

generator was disconnected as the field windings were 'meggered' to find the fault. Fury reigns over the workmanship of B.R.E.L Doncaster works quality control. Spirits were at a low ebb as all the man hours and the dedication of the Laira fitters and electricians came to nothing. Oh well, that's life with Class 50s. All will have to be done again when an overhauled main generator carcass for the locomotive arrives from Doncaster works.

On 8th December 1982, 50034 'Furious', now in Large Logo livery, came onto Laira depot with low power. Many faults were sorted out even though it had only been one month since the loco was refurbished at Doncaster works. On this day 'Furious' was booked to assist 1M85 07.40 Penzance -Liverpool from Plymouth, but returned to Laira a failure suffering from power earth faults. Once again the main generator had an earth fault on the field windings and so arrangements were made to return 50034 to Doncaster works - yet again!

On the 15th December, a decision was made that 50034 was to be repaired at Laira depot- oh no! The gangs once again got ready to strip out and lift the power unit as a new main generator was coming from Doncaster works by road. By 7th January 1983, 50034 is completed once again and worked the IV76, the 09.20 ex-Liverpool-Penzance. 50034's next visit to Laira was for its `F` Exam and a full re—paint into Network South East livery and this was on 9th December 1986. In later years a 50 tonne

overhead crane was erected in number five and six roads at Laira depot for Class 50 Power Units to be exchanged inside .... and in the warm. Life with the Class 50s certainly had its ups and downs!

The Bishops Triple

Neil Reed, Manager — "Fancy a Bishops Triple'?"
Ian Harris, Fitter `C` shift- "Don't mind if I do"
Martin Bennett, Electrician `B` shift - "I`ll have a pint"
Neil Reed, Manager — "No you fools, it's a tour to York with three Class 50s".

It is Saturday 5th June 1993. 'The Bishops Triple' was a railtour from Minehead to York organised by Pathfinder Tours in conjunction with the West Somerset Railway. The object was to take Laira`s flagship Class 50, 50007 'Sir Edward Elgar' to York, where it was to spend the summer in the National Railway Museum. As usual the three Class Fifties were prepared in the week prior to the tour with 50007 receiving an extra coat of paint and a polish, another Laira speciality.

Departure time from Laira was 02.15... .what a time to book on duty at 01.30. Arriving for duty the three trustee steeds were found in number two road, batteries on charge and ready for the days jaunt up the East Coast mainline. After the driver had carried out his brake tests, etc., it was then time to take them outside for the final top up of fuel and

50033 in Network Southeast Livery, D400 in BR blue and Green 50007 wait with their crew to work the return leg of the Bishop's Triple railtour in the York Holding Sidings. Dicky Daw, Geoff Hudson, Martin Bennett and Ian Harris. Photo Mike Woodhouse

coolant. It is a long way from Plymouth to York and back, some five hundred and fifty six miles or so. Ian Harris and Martin Bennett gave all three locomotives the 'once over', after which they were ready for the departure time of 02.15 from Laira depot.

All forty eight cylinders of English Electric power came into life as they made their way to Exeter. After a crew change here, they had to go to Taunton to collect a shunter pilot to take them through Taunton Cider Brewery sidings.

After collecting the pilot they set off for a short trip into the jungle sidings at Taunton.

They then had to set back through the Taunton Cider Brewery siding where they then gained access to the West Somerset Railway line at Norton Fitzwarren. They travelled on this line as far as Bishops Lydeard station where they were to pick up the train. This arrived from Minehead behind a black 8 , an 8F Class LMS steam locomotive, with the stock formed of the 'Pilkington' set, a rake of twelve privately sponsored BR Mark l coaches in a multicoloured liveried paint scheme. Coupling up to the stock and changing from vacuum to air, the full brake test was carried out.

Departure from Bishops Lydeard was at 07.25, fifteen minutes late, but Bristol Temple Meads station was reached only five minutes down. There the railtour fans were loaded, the whistle blown and the 1241 powered its way north.

Photographers were waiting at every bridge and

any available space was filled with stills cameras and video cameras, particularly as the railtour started to climb the 'Lickey incline' where it must have been a sight to behold as all three Class 50s were working in multiple for the first time. 8,000hp storming up a one in forty two incline at 60mph — good even by HST standards. They travelled through the suburbs of Birmingham, now under the wires, which had only been energised that very day around the Camp Hill avoiding line, and out to Saltley for a crew change.

Then it was up the Midland main line to Derby, where Ian and Martin had a chance to chat with an ex-Laira fitter (they just can't stay away from these Class 50s), before the tour set off to Sheffield. On this leg there were more photographers, even on the trackside who were trespassing on the railway to obtain their valuable shots. The train travelled around the avoiding line which passes Booth's scrap yard where many scrapped locomotives could be seen from a distance, including several Class 50s which was a sad sight to observe. From Doncaster the three 50s were under the wires again on the East Coast for the remainder of the journey to York which was reached on time at 13.00.

Dicky Daw, Electrician `A` shift, and myself Fitter `B` shift were standing at York station on platform 9 awaiting the arrival of the 'Bishops Triple'. It arrived on time having made its journey with no troubles. The only one job left to do now was to uncouple 50007 'Sir Edward Elgar' (which was leading the train) before it ran light engine to the nearby Clifton sidings to be duly handed over to the care of the National Railway Museum for the summer. After shunting, D400 'Fearless' and 50033 'Glorious' were stood down to await the return trip. Ian and Martin made their way to the hotel, which was fit for a king (Queen Victoria had stayed there once). A well earned rest was called for, following a very long day after an early start. The two remaining Class 50s — D400 'Fearless and 50033 'Glorious' — were now in the hands of Dicky and myself for the return leg home of lZ4l 16.50 York-Minehead, 'Bishops Triple'. But that's another story!

Summertime Special: National Railway Museum, 1993

Sunday 29th August 1993, Bank Holiday weekend and a journey to the National Railway Museum at York to bring home to the Western Region 50007 'Sir Edward Elgar' after being on display in the Great Hall over the past three months.

Sunday afternoon, whilst awaiting the arrival at Plymouth station of a Penzance — Edinburgh HST service, Martin Bennett and I take a call from Swindon control. The engine on the rear power car (43123) had shut down and we were asked to assist once we had boarded the train on its way north. The fault was found en-route and we had rectified it by the time we arrived at Exeter St Davids station. On arrival at York station we were taken to the Viking Hotel to book in for the night. We then received a message from the N.R.M management about the arrangements for the following morning, Bank Holiday Monday. After a good night's sleep and a hearty breakfast, we walked to the National

Railway Museum in Leeman Road and made our way to meet Richard Gibbons, Head of Engineering and his colleague, Ray Towell.

When we arrived shortly after 09.45, Green 50007 was standing amongst the exhibits, including 4-4-0 G.W.R 3440 'City of Truro'. Our job was to examine `07 for its journey home to the British Rail depot at Laira. With overalls on, we towed `07 out from the museum with Class 02 0-4-0 D2860 and put her on the inspection pit beside green liveried Class 40 D200. A full examination of 50007 was made and, after barring the engine round, the start button was depressed. Happily `07 burst back into life and the battery charging and running lamps were checked. We left `07 to warm up whilst we had a coffee behind the scenes of the main hall. A driver then arrived to take 50007 light engine to Leeds Holbeck depot for fuel. As we sat there, green liveried 47833 of Bristol Bath Road powered its way north with Pathfinder's 'The North Yorkshireman Explorer' railtour from London Paddington to York and Scarborough. It would be the return of this train that 50007 would work south so it could restart its normal duties.

At 13.30 we passed through the gates of the N.R.M en-route to Leeds, to run via Castleford. At 13.32 we got the road onto the ECML. Class 91 91011 to London Kings Cross passed south into platform 11 while DMU 158909, in South Yorkshire livery, had just arrived. Selby coalmine was passed with its shaft pithead and winding gear pointing skyward as we ran light at 20mph. Ferrybridge Power Station cooling towers then dominated the skyline. The Yorkshire countryside was lovely and in full sunshine, as harvesting was taking place along the route making it a pleasant sight. Castleford was reached where the sharp curves made `07s wheels

50007 on display beside the turntable in National Railway Museum at York. Photo: Paul Furtek

screech. The area still had upper quadrant signals and the local signalman gave us a wave as a Class 50 is a rare sight in this area. Methley and Stourton signal boxes were passed as we neared Leeds. At Hunslet, Class 323 body shells were seen on accommodation bogies and we were told this works was to close in five weeks time.

As we entered Leeds Holbeck depot servicing shed it became evident that it was the opposite of Laira, being very old, black, oily and dirty. 50007 'Sir Edward Elgar' had a brush up of its windows, a top up of oils and coolant. 1,325 litres of fuel were also taken on board so there was just enough time for me to take a quick photograph. At 15.00 we crawled out to the dummy signal at Holbeck to await the road back to York, this time travelling via Neville Hill. We left Leeds via Central station passing Neville Hill depot, the main Inter-City route into Leeds. The outward journey to Leeds took 45 minutes but it was only 25 minutes back to York. What a difference a route makes!

We stabled 50007 on Clifton holding sidings while shunting D200 into the museum in place of `07 using D2860. 50007 was started up at 17.45 before running light engine to Holgate sidings to await the 1Z44 return charter. However, signal YK211 had a fault, which although did not affect InterCity services, meant that we had to telephone the signalman to release our locomotive to platform 3. On arriving at York station the 50 attached to the front of the 1244 as the pilot locomotive. The train was now double-headed with two green locomotives — 50007 and 47833. The whistle was blown and `07 took power again leaving York ten minutes late. We headed the 'North Yorkshireman Explorer' south into the setting sun with two green Western Region locomotives trying to make up time along the East Coast mainline under the wires. 1Z44 retraced its northbound route with the BN95 coaching stock. After a successful run to Reading, `07 was detached from the train at just past midnight. A fresh loco crew had arrived from Exeter to take 50007, our taxi, light engine home to Laira.

Tuesday 31st August 1993 at 00.25 saw 50007 set off from Reading for Plymouth. Arrival at Laira was at 04.21 after which it was home to bed. Although very tired and hungry we would do it all again given the opportunity, such was life with the remaining Class 50s in service with BR.

Project Defiance 50149: Judgment Day - 18th August 1993

It is Wednesday 18th August 1993 and it's a beautiful summer's day. My eldest son, Simon, and I went ahead early to Laira for the final preparation for the days big event at the depot — the re—dedication of 50149 'Defiance'. Simon joined the

main party on 50149 which was stabled in Lipson number five siding, awaiting a tow to the main depot. My own duties were to prepare 50033 'Glorious' and D400 'Fearless' for the Laira line up, which was now part of Depot Engineer Malcolm Wishart's remit.

At 10.30, 50149 'Defiance', resplendent in two-tone Railfreight grey with hand painted 'Railfreight General' decals, was towed into position outside Laira number three road for the ceremony where the dais and freshly ironed navy curtains were fitted across the nameplate.

Guests were starting to arrive and introductions were duly made while flowers for the guests wives were delivered.

Our Area Fleet Manager, Geoff Hudson, welcomed everyone and then proceeded to join all the guests and assembled photographers. At just after 11.00, the invited guests made their way to the dais ready for the unveiling of 50149. Our chairman, Mr David Clough of Project Defiance, opened the proceedings by speaking of the purchase and the history of our acquisition before handing over to Geoff Hudson. In his address he paid tribute to the dedication of the volunteers of Project Defiance. He then introduced Captain Walker of HMS Defiance, Devonport Naval Base. Captain Walker spoke of the name 'Defiance' and the similarity of older Warships requiring pure dedication and money to keep them going, as was the case with his team of Royal Navy servicemen.

After all the speeches, the special guests' wives received their bouquets and 50149 'Defiance' was duly unveiled. The start up of 50149 was then orchestrated by our conductor, Malcolm Wishart, along with D400 'Fearless' and 50033 'Glorious' for a photographic session.

To end this final event there was a toast to 'Defiance' followed by light refreshments which were served for everybody.

50149 has not been reverted to its freight configuration as it retains its 100mph bogies and not the CP12 bogies it had temporarily fitted for the Railfreight trials that limited it to 80mph running. On Saturday 21st August, 50149 was put on show at Laira before its journey eastwards to its new home. Movement from Laira to the Worksop Open Day to be held on 5th September 1993 commenced at 07.45 on 25th August when it was towed by a Res-liveried Class 47, number 47568 'Royal Engineers Postal and Courier Services', to Exeter Riverside yard on the first leg of its journey.

For the next leg, 37138 from the Trainload Metals sector was attached to haul 50149 to Westbury where it stabled overnight. At lunchtime the next day our travelling escorts were back at Westbury for the evening departure to Swindon to make the next connection to Bescot. This was a short journey

The rededication of 50149 to HMS Defiance. L-R Geoff Hudson, Captain Walker (of HMS Defiance), Malcolm Wishart, Chris Holland, and David Clough. Photo: Mike Woodhouse

behind 37174. After a layover of around three hours, the civil engineers train ran on time to Bescot yard with 47300 taking over for the onward journey to Toton yard.

On the Friday at Toton yard, many other locos were assembled for onward movement to Worksop for the open day. Light engine movements were now the order of the day and 50149 was one of them. Thousands attended the British Rail Trainload Coal Open Day at Worksop, Nottinghamshire, on 5th September 1993 where 50149 'Defiance' was one of the stars of the show. Large crowds gathered around the loco throughout the day and it's unique livery ensured that endless photographs were taken of her. After the doors had closed to the public, 'Defiance' left Worksop at 18.30 along with other locos destined for South Wales and 50149 later arrived at its new home of Allied Steel and Wire at Cardiff. One final appearance in 1993 was at the Newport Rail Day where once again 50149 was the only privately preserved locomotive on display, as all other exhibited locos were from British Rail sectors.

Today, 50149 is in safe hands in preservation although it has now reverted to 50049 and is in Large Logo livery following a re-paint at Cardiff in the summer of 2010. Incidentally, it's bogies which it had as 50149 in BR days are now under 37003 — which is also in preservation.

Update: 50049 is now mainline certified and over the last twenty five years has visited almost all corners of the UK's rail network. Currently 'Defiance' is in GBRf's blue and orange livery reflecting their use of the loco on their contracted work.

Val's Curtain Call

During the rundown of the Class 50s a good friend of mine, Paul Furtek of Locomaster Profiles, decided to capture the last few years of the Class 50s on video. On his many visits to see Geoff Hudson, Area Fleet Manager of Laira depot, he would normally call in on me at home in Ivybridge for a cuppa and a chat. On this particular afternoon, with a Devon welcome, we discussed an opening sequence for his latest video production, 'Rise and Fall of the 50s'.

My dear wife Val was also involved in the discussion. In conversation Paul made mention of an idea he had but did not think possible to achieve. The idea was to have a Class 50 bursting through some sort of a banner for the opening sequence. Val had some thoughts and suggested using some high quality special paper to use as a screen for the locomotive to be driven through, therefore achieving the effect required. This was going to be quite a challenge, mainly due to its size but all three of us thought it was a great idea .... if we could pull it off! Paul said he would discuss the idea with Geoff at Laira but we were all mindful that this would have to be done without interruption to the depot and its heavy workload. A few days later Paul got the O.K from Geoff and so some detailed planning now had to be done. Laira's Number six road was selected. Measurements and other notes taken such as which part of the locomotive would come through the banner first. This would be the buffers, so measurements were taken from rail height. It was decided that the Class 50 would not be running as air draft and exhaust smoke would be a problem. A Class 08 diesel electric shunting locomotive would therefore be inside the shed to gently push the Class 50 out of the shed and through the banner. The trick was to have the paper banner tear easily and in the right place. Thoughts then turned to designing and getting the paper banner made. This was going to be some challenge but our determination took over. We have a paper mill in Ivybridge, just down the road from where we live. Wiggins Teape supplied top quality paper and among their many customers were the Bank of England, mainly for bank notes. Val thought that because of our special requirements the paper mill would be a good starting place. So a telephone call for help and information was made. On our visit to the paper mill we found them very helpful when we explained to them what we wanted to use the paper for. This was a request they had never had before and they were most probably thinking we were slightly mad. Nonetheless, they were more than willing to help.

The paper mill came up trumps. Following a production run of the finest thick durable white paper on a solid cardboard roll, there was some that was surplus to requirements. All they asked for was a small donation — great! The collection was arranged but there was a slight difficulty — we had to transport it by fitting it into an Austin Maestro hatchback!! This was just about managed and the paper roll was safely brought home.

The next job was to source where we could get the printing done. Out came the Yellow Pages which we scanned for printers that could possibly do the job and we eventually settled on a small company in Plymouth's Barbican area. A visit was made to their premises, where we discussed what we wanted done. We were asking a lot from them as they were only a small printing firm and it proved to be the largest-area printing request they had ever had.

Well, it was after all the size of a locomotive shed door! So much so that its size would only just be able to be accommodated on their bench areas. However, they came up trumps for us and were not only willing to do the job but I think they enjoyed the challenge.

At the next meeting with Paul he produced a picture of a Laira depot logo with the words 'Locomaster Profiles Presents' painted in blue and laid out as he required for the opening scene. Late one afternoon, Geoff, Malcolm, Val and I gathered together in one of the Laira classrooms. We moved all the chairs and rolled out the paper that was to be the shed door.

Gosh — it was large and it completely filled the room. We needed to mark out the buffer heights with dotted lines as well as the other sections that needed to give way when the locomotive came into contact with the banner — i.e. the roof line height etc. This was achieved by making perforations on the banner so that they would easily give way to the slightest pressure. This had to be done carefully to achieve the desired result, especially as there would only be one attempt at this. The measurements were made and marked and then

50033's breakthrough into the open sequence of Locomaster Profile's programme: 50 Terminator. Photo: Mike Woodhouse

they were checked and rechecked. It had to be correct and there was no room for error either. Allowances also had to be made for the fixing of the banner — if these were wrong this would throw all the height measurements as well as the perforations for the 'burst through' points.

Once all these measurements were marked out, the next task was to take the roll of paper to the printers for the sign writing and the Laira logo to be done. The printers were also going to put the perforations in the correct places, thus ensuring a clean break of the banner when the Class 50 burst through it.

Ten days later the printer rang to say the roll was finished and it was awaiting collection. When we arrived to collect it the gentleman showed us the finished article and they had made a great job of it- it looked really good. He laughed at what we were trying to achieve, thinking it would be a near impossible task. As it happened he was the son of one of my `B` shift supervisors at the time and he asked us to let him know how it all went after our event. It certainly was a very different commission. Our Austin Maestro was once again at the ready and was loaded nervously with the precious roll. Now it was back to the Laira classroom for storage. At Laira the whole paper curtain, which was now cut to the actual required size, was rolled out and all the perforation marks were checked ready for the big day. Thoughts came to us as to how difficult this was going to be when hanging it into place in the shed doorway.

We knew this would be a daunting task with the through draft that was always present in the shed. Hopefully the good quality paper would ensure that there would be no damage. Val had done many things before but never anything quite like this! It was now up to Geoff Hudson and Malcolm Wishart to organise the Class 50 and a Class 08 and arrange for the hanging of the large paper banner inside the steel roller door on number 6 road. Geoff arranged the time for mid-afternoon, after I had completed my early turn duty and Val had finished work at the local college. Colleagues from the Outdoor Machinery Department were on hand with their cherry picker hoist to attach the paper banner in place. After the Class 08 diesel shunter had towed 50033 'Glorious' into place just inside the shed, the roller door was then slowly closed. Val, myself and Depot Engineer Malcolm Wishart arrived from the classroom armed with the paper banner on the roll for installing. Depot staff gathered round to watch in amazement to see what was going on. Malcolm Wishart commented to Paul that "this is a locomotive maintenance depot, not a Hollywood film studio". This caused a laugh, lightening the tension as the task began with difficulty, due to the height and the through draft which we knew was going to be a problem. We had

to be very careful not to allow all our hard work to be ruined before it was even installed. We commenced the positioning of this paper door carefully, bit by bit, and finally it was hung into place with only a small tear. There was a big sigh of relief all round as this stage of the project was now completed.

Paul, his tripod and video cameras were set up outside in the locomotive yard. Two way radios were now at the ready. The plan was for the shed door to raise to reveal the banner and then for 50033 to be pushed through it. As I mentioned earlier, there could only be the one take, so we had to get it right. The go ahead for the steel roller door to open was given but there was a strong easterly wind blowing. The paper banner started to push inward and so an immediate halt was given to opening the roller door any further.

It was decided to get the Class 08 to ease up and push the Class 50 as close to the paper banner as possible, thus closing the gap and to hold its weight. Surely it would not all go wrong at this stage. There was a pause in the wind and the words GO, GO, GO came over the radio. The metal shed door rolled upwards and 50033 'Glorious' edged its way forward and successfully tore through the paper banner — exactly as we wanted. Phew! Paul captured this sequence perfectly on video, the buffer lines tore evenly and everyone was relieved that all the hard work and planning had paid off. All were overjoyed with this success. Paul's initial idea had been fulfilled, and Val's curtain call lived up to its name. The result is there for all to see as the opening sequence on Locomaster Profiles '50 Terminator' DVD.

Geoff's Dream

To take two Class 50s in 1960s 'as built' livery back to Glasgow via Settle and Carlisle, over Beattock summit, and return via the West Coast mainline. 'The Midland Scotsman': lZ42 06.58 Birmingham New Street- Glasgow Central would do this with a load of eleven coaches or 455 tonnes.

5th February 1994, sunshine, Class 50s and magic are the ingredients of the day. This was to be the pinnacle of the final Class 50 railtours under British Rail control. The whistle is blown and power is taken as the lZ42 winds its way out of Birmingham New Street station.

At this stage I am riding in the rear cab of Class 50 D400. An hourly check around the engine room will be needed en—route to Glasgow and return to check oil pressure, turbo charger pressure, oil, fuel and coolant. Exhaust leaks will also be examined as will the charge rate of the batteries whilst on the move. Wearing ear defenders is a must when in the engine room while these examinations are taking place.

As we head up the West Coast mainline a pick-up stop is made at Stafford. My two sons and friends from the Exeter area are waiting on the platform to join the train at 07.40. Having driven through the night, these likely lads were also out for a memorable trip with these two blue British Rail Class 50s.

Our two Class 50s settled down to a steady jaunt over metals that were once familiar to them, as when built these machines were used regularly on the Crewe-Glasgow West Coast mainline to accelerate the late 1960's timetable.

At Lostock Hall junction we slowed to take the curve for Blackbum. Our Class 50s then crawled through the station and into the tunnel before taking the freight only line to Clitheroe via Daisyfield junction. This was new territory for our locomotive crew and maintenance staff. At Hellifield we joined the Settle and Carlisle route at its southern end where the 1Z42 with its 5,400hp began to attack the challenging route. Another look round of D400 takes place as I will go onto the leading locomotive D433 after the Appleby stop for the remainder of the journey into Scotland. Soon the train was powering through Ribblehead station and onto the famous viaduct which was built between 1870/1875 by the Midland Railway. The viaduct, with its twenty four stone arches, came into view. The last Class 50s over this stretch of route were 50018/37/46 which were en-route to M.C. Metals in Glasgow for breaking. The awe inspiring structure dominates the landscape in this part of the Pennines and is a monumental achievement to the navvies who laboured to build it.

All too quickly the two British Rail blue locomotives, D400 and D433, are making a triumphant return to the Cumberland Fells, echoing that wonderful magic English Electric sound, before passing through Blea Moor tunnel and over the top of Dentdale and Garsdale and entering the lush surrounds of the Eden Valley. A stop was made at Appleby where passengers who wished to alight from the train had to do so from the first three coaches, due to the eleven coach length of the train. The train then reversed and made a run past on full power, ideal for photographers but even better for those with video cameras. The train reversed again through the station for a second run past. This was the first time that this had been attempted on a BR operated modern traction railtour. The passengers

then boarded the train again before the 1Z42 continued its journey north. The Settle and Carlisle was also used by many Class 50s in the early days on regular diagrammed freight services, one of which was the 7V00 Carlisle Kingmoor-St. Blazey and the 7M86 St. Blazey—Carlisle Kingmoor service. Having changed locomotives to D433, I watched as we came off the Settle-Carlisle route at Petteril Bridge junction and proceeded into Carlisle station for a crew change. Refreshments were taken and at 12.57 we got the road for the 'Midland Scotsman's' sprint from England and over the border into Scotland. We passed Gretna junction and the climb seems no effort as we head up to Beattock summit at a height of 1,015 feet above sea

In the fading light available at Glasgow Central a lone piper stands between D400 and D433 to mark the last trip to Scotland by a pair of BR class 50s. Photo: Mike Woodhouse

level. This is one of Geoff 's favourite places along this route, so he must be a happy man. Beattock summit is the spot where on 18th May 1969, 400 sustained heavy number one cab damage whilst working 1S07 21.30 Euston-Glasgow sleeper. Happily, today D400 is in fine form and performing well.

We slow on the approach to Glasgow Central station, where orange liveried EMU's and DMU's are seen. Photographers are everywhere as we come to rest on the stop blocks at the end of platform nine. Even one of our Laira colleagues has come along to video the scene in his home city whilst staying with his sister.

A short speech is made by Geoff Hudson while our stock is drawn out to Polmadie for servicing. Our two Class 50s then ran light engine to Motherwell diesel depot. There, my mate Dicky

Daw and I changed over the headboard from D433 to D400 for the return journey.

Oils, coolant and fuel were checked again and topped up as required while all the locomotive's windscreens were cleaned ready for the return run. A comment was made by Scottish Traction Inspector John Thompson that he never thought he would ever see two Class 50s in British Rail blue, back on Motherwell depot.

How wrong he was! Both locomotives were restarted and we retraced our way back to Glasgow Central station to rejoin the railtour stock for our return leg back to Birmingham New Street station. Hundreds of people had gathered round as a Scottish 'Dalskeith Piper' nostalgically played 'Amazing Grace'. Then, at 17.03 our two Class 50s, with D400 leading this time, sadly departed Glasgow Central station to the tune of Auld Lang Syne. What a way to say goodbye! This time the train headed straight down the West Coast main line as the daylight began to fade. The sights and sounds of the last eighteen hours would remain with us all forever.

Stafford was reached at 21.50 where I waved goodbye to my two sons as they left the train to make their way back home to the West Country. Our two Class 50s continued on their last leg, whisking us through the darkness of the suburbs of Birmingham. As we trundle the last few miles towards New Street, we all reflected on the day's events and what a successful railtour it had been. Geoff's dream of taking two Class 50s in British Rail blue livery to Glasgow had been accomplished but was now drawing to a close as we pulled into Birmingham New Street station at 23.00. We headed off to our hotel ready for a night cap with thoughts of a magnificent day out. If the 50019 inquiry was the lowest point of my railway career, then this was the highlight.

Glorious - Against All Odds

D433 was delivered brand new from the Vulcan Foundry of the English Electric Company at Newton-le-Willows to British Rail's Crewe diesel depot 20th July 1968. At this point it was just another D400 (later to become Class 50) in standard Rail blue livery but, over the next forty five years, it would turn into something of a celebrity.

In May 1974, it left the London Midland Region at Crewe and was transferred to Bristol Bath Road depot on the Western Region. In October 1976 it was transferred again, this time to Plymouth Laira. I was given the task of fitting the 'Glorious' nameplates to the locomotive on 26th June 1978. At this time the locomotive was undergoing maintenance at Laira. It was the 37th class 50 to be named. HMS GLORIOUS was a aircraft carrier deployed to protect the WWII arctic convoys.

In September 1979, 50033 was transferred away to Old Oak Common and, while it was based there, it entered Doncaster works for a general overhaul and refurbishment. On 15th October 1981, 50033 'Glorious' emerged from Doncaster in Large Logo livery and returned to Old Oak Common as the twenty second Class 50 to be refurbished. In 1985, 50033 entered Doncaster works for a second time, this time for an intermediate overhaul. After the work was completed it returned to Old Oak Common on the 10th September 1985.

In June 1986 Network SouthEast came into being and so began a process of re-painting locomotives and coaching stock into a new livery. At the turn of the decade in early 1990, 50033 was stopped at its home depot of Old Oak Common for a power unit change and a full re-paint into Network South East darker blue (3) livery. Although at this point it belonged to the NWRA fleet, it was not one of the seventeen Class 50s selected to receive an `F exam at Laira. In January 1990 the nameplates were lowered and aligned to the middle of the body, thus reading 'Glorious Network SouthEast'. It was then confirmed that Old Oak would lose its remaining Class 50s from the NWRA 'Thames & Chiltern Fleet', with the locos being replaced by 47/4 and 47/7's in May 1990.

The nine Old Oak Common Class 50s were then transferred to Laira depot with 50033 'Glorious' being one of them. A decision was then taken as to which, if any, of them, were to be replaced by examples currently in the NSSA Waterloo-Exeter route fleet. Either way, it looked like a blood bath was on the cards unless a costly life-extension program for the Class was forthcoming. I wondered if 50033 would get through this rocky period as six Class 50s were to be withdrawn in just six weeks. In September 1990, with 50033 now allocated to Laira, the loco required two new wheel sets and it was decided that it would receive both bogies from withdrawn 50032 'Courageous'. The work was carried out and 50033 ready to return to traffic. Network SouthEast had been concerned with the significant fluctuation in the availability of the Class 50s and there were rumours that all of the Class could be withdrawn on 8th July 1991. Fortunately these rumours proved to be groundless. During May, a line up of the Laira Class 50s with D400, 50007, 50008, 50015, and 50031 was staged for Rail Magazine.

Although 50033 did not feature, there was still time for another star to be born. But would it be 50029, 50030, or 50033? For the Laira Open Day on 15th September 1991, 50033 was on the depot with several other classmates as it required a traction motor change. This was completed by 20th September. A railtour duty followed as a third Class 50 was needed as back-up on 23rd November, when 50033 assisted the 'Valiant Thunderer' railtour (with 50008 and 50015) from Plymouth to Newquay and return. All three locos powered the return leg to Bristol Temple Meads station before returning light to Laira. 50015 and 50008 were both withdrawn on arrival back at the depot.

Sandite duties followed for 50033 which worked from St. Blazey yard to Newton Abbot over the South Devon banks, spraying the rail heads with Sandite (a railhead adhesion compound) from a former DMU driving trailer. On 20th December, after the autumn leaf-fall season had finished, 50033's nameplates were removed and placed in secure storage at Laira, ready for sending to Collectors Corner for sale. 50033 was put into store but, although it was operational, it was suffering a badly smoking power unit. By 18th January 1992 a decision to retain 50030, 50033 and D400 had been made and even though 50033's power unit gave cause for concern, repairs had been agreed. Eight new cylinder heads, five new pistons and one cylinder liner were supplied to rectify the problem, and it became my job over the next week or so to carry out the necessary repairs. During this time 'Glorious' was given a full re-paint and had its nameplates refitted. Thus, another scrape with the Grim Reaper had been avoided. On 3rd April 1992, the loco underwent a test run from Laira to Bristol with a rake of TPO stock. 50033 performed faultlessly and was therefore successfully back to traffic.

On the weekend of 23/24th May 1992, I was on duty at Laira on the early shift. My job that day was to service 50033 for its last day in traffic for Network South East. I asked the depots management if 50033 could run under a 75mph restriction instead of the usual 100mph to help prevent any failure. After a telephone call to headquarters at Swindon via headquarters at Waterloo, a resounding 'NO' came back. The reason given for this was that, as the loco was in active service, it had to keep to the train service timings. While at home that evening I received a telephone call to say 'Glorious' had failed with a 'flashover' at Basingstoke on the 14.22 Exeter-Waterloo service. The train had to be terminated and this in itself caused considerable disruption to other train services.

Would 50033 survive this time? That depended on how bad the damage was. After the locomotive was towed back to Laira it was inspected by Dicky Daw who would assess whether 'Glorious' could be repaired as it appeared that the main generator and all six traction motors had suffered 'flashover' damage. Over the next couple of days 50033's future hung in the balance but in the end repairs were carried out and the loco returned to traffic for the third time. This time though, a 75mph restriction was put in place so that it could continue on railtours, working in multiple with the other remaining 50s.

'Glorious' was a popular loco and it featured on many of the Class 50 railtours. At this time the National Railway Museum at York were interested in claiming a Class 50 for their collection. Consideration was given to all three locos - D400, 50007 and 50033. It had already been suggested that 'Glorious' would be ideal for the York collection on several accounts- namely that it was in good running order and that it's present Network SouthEast livery reflected the guise in which the locomotive ended its British Rail career. A meeting was called by Geoff Hudson (AFM at Laira) who invited railtour operator Peter Watts of Pathfinder Tours, Paul Furtek of Locomaster Profiles and some of Laira's management to discuss and plan out the final trains that the remaining British Rail Class 50s would work. Geoff was keen to maximise the farewell railtour program to include routes that the 50s had worked over in their 35 years of service. He asked those at the meeting for comments. Peter Watts was keen to run the last railtour in British Rail ownership and it was suggested that the final tour was to be called the '50 Terminator'. This would run from London Waterloo to Exeter and Penzance and then return into London Paddington as these routes were all associated with the Class 50s while they were under Geoff 's command at Laira.

Geoff himself suggested that any farewell program should include a trip to Glasgow — with a

50033 with matching stock runs down Rattery Bank with the 1340 Plymouth Portsmouth service. Photo: Simon Woodhouse

50033 looking resplendent waits in the National Railway Museum car park prior to its grand entrance and acceptance into the museum's collection. Photo: Mike Woodhouse

matching pair of Rail blue liveried 50s, 1960's style, storming over Beattock summit. If 50033 could be re-painted back into Rail blue livery as D433 so that it could pair up with sister locomotive D400, it would make for one hell of a nostalgic trip to Glasgow. Having been completely sold on the idea, the opportunity of turning the clock back twenty five years was quite simply irresistible; furthermore, it would be the last chance to do this with British Rail owned Class 50s.

Within forty eight hours Geoff had agreed with Paul that Locomaster Profiles would fund the one-off re-paint and so Geoff was able to start planning the restoration schedule with work starting on 50033 by the end of that week. The transformation of 50033 was to take just under three weeks. It became evident just how momentous this task was, as not only was there extensive time consuming repairs to 50033's bodywork, but the depot also had an exceptionally busy work schedule with many HST vehicles undergoing repairs. As a result, it is worth recording here that Geoff Hudson and Depot Engineer Malcolm Wishart really pulled out all the stops to get the work completed, without disrupting the Inter—City work. As if that were not enough, we even managed to re—paint D400 in time for the unveiling of D433 at Laira on 29th January so that both locos were in ex—works condition. The two immaculate Class 50s, which were placed side by side outside the workshop, erupted to produce one of the most spectacular start-ups ever seen. The re—paint of D433 was particularly special as the locomotive will only run in this guise for one day only — on the Class 40 Appeal's 'Midland Scotsman'. Who would have thought, back in the autumn of 1991 when

Glorious' was apparently working out its last days on Sandite duties, that this machine would survive to the very end and eventually into the national collection?

After the 'The Midland Scotsman' railtour to Glasgow, the nameless D433 returned to Laira to undergo further body restoration work and a full repaint into British Rail Large Logo livery and numbered as 50033. In keeping with this guise, she was again reunited with her 'Glorious' nameplates which would stay with her for her two remaining railtours. These last tours would be the 'Cornish Caper' and 'The Glorious Sunset', the second of which would see 50033 work from York to Scarborough and return, prior to being handed over to the National Railway Museum.

Good Friday of the Easter weekend in 1994, and 50033 'Glorious' entered the Great Hall of the National Railway Museum to a fanfare of detonators and smoke to a huge audience gathered round the turntable. On behalf of British Rail, Geoff Hudson formally handed the locomotive over to Andrew Dow, the Curator of the Museum. Short speeches were made and 50033 happily passed into a secure future. Arguably one of the most popular Class 50s but I must report that 50033 was later sidelined by the NRM, and after a short spell at Steam in Swindon she was stored at Tyseley in Birmingham awaiting a new home. — 'GOODBYE GLORIOUS'

Update: In 2017 the management team at Tyseley approached the Class 50 Alliance to see if an agreement could be reached to have 50033 repaired and returned to use. Under this agreement Glorious made its return at the Severn Valley Railway's 50s at 50 Gala in 2018.

The Finale of Class 50s on British Rail

Riding the '50 Terminator'
1Z40 08.52 Waterloo-Exeter St. Davids
26th March 1994

There's a beautiful golden sunrise over Clapham junction yard in south west London as we prepare the two Class 50s for their final run in British Rail service. Once, Clapham was a very busy yard but it now stands quiet and empty of diesel locomotives, except for 50007 ' Sir Edward Elgar' and 50050 'Fearless' . At 06.30 our Laira team along with Traction Inspector Graham Petre, Driver Tony Kowalewki and Paul Furtek of Locomaster Profiles arrive to board our two Class 50s in readiness for Pathfinder Tours grand finale railtour, the '50 Terminator', from London Waterloo to London Paddington via Penzance, thus bringing together all three termini once visited by the Class 50s.

A full check of both locomotive's oil, coolant and fuel levels takes place before both 50s are fired up. Both locomotives are then checked for battery charge and pre—power tests are undertaken from each cab. With both locos now ready, we hand over the two 50s to the Salisbury driver who will take us on the first leg of the railtour. Meanwhile Paul Furtek has set up his filming equipment with a specially fitted microphone to record the locomotives when under power. This is the first time that something like this has been attempted and is the result of considerable planning. Our driver walked to the control cabin in the main yard at Clapham to release the locomotives so we could run light engine to Waterloo. At 07 .30 we were waved down to the dummy signal by the yard shunter supervisor.

An EMU passed by us going into Waterloo, then the point work ahead of us switched over. The dummy signal changed, we took power and our Class 50s eased towards Waterloo.

We had been informed by telephone in the cab that the two Class 50s will be stabled in the next platform to that of our train until departure time so that photographers can take their pictures. This was because our train will be a ten coach set plus 47484 'Isambard Kingdom Brunel' which was hauling the empty stock into the terminus. The two Class 50s would have fouled the platform, so until arrival of the stock people were able to photograph the two immaculate Laira Class 50s under Waterloo's famous station roof.

Many regular faces were seen as the Laira team met many acquaintances who had supported the Class 50s on the railtours during the last couple of years. One person brought along a wreath of laurel leaves saying "Farewell" which was placed over 50007 first, and then 50050 for photographs. After that, the '50 Terminator' headboard was firmly fixed in readiness for the journey. Coffee was taken while the empty stock of the railtour train arrived into the adjacent platform behind GWR green liveried 47484 'IKB'. The 47 had hauled the stock from Norwich Crown Point and it comprised ten Bounds Green based Mark II air conditioned coaches.

The platform supervisor was now ready for us to join the train (headcoded lZ40) which would take us over the South Western route to Exeter. As our two Class 50s were restarted under the roof, railway personnel were watching from the control centre which is situated above the station concourse. This would be the last time they would see such a sight. The signal was given and we ran through the point work of the throat of Waterloo station and then backed onto the stock. With the minutes to departure time ticking away, a brake test is made and the ETH (electric train heat) supply was switched on. Finally, with 50050 leading, we were ready for the first 172.12 miles to Exeter St David`s.

At 08.52 the guard waved us away in bright sunshine and the crowds watched as 50007 and 50050 powered the '50 Terminator' out of platform nine. 60mph was quickly reached running on single or double yellow signals through Clapham junction station. There, 73136 'Kent Youth Orchestra' was stabled in the yard. Wimbledon was then passed at the trains maximum permitted speed of 75mph after which power was shut off as the AWS siren blew.

We were now running on double yellows at 60mph. On the approach to Woking the brakes were applied for a red signal ahead, but as it changed to a single yellow, power was taken so that the train ambled at 25mph under a caution aspect. A route 91 bus — the bread van type - overtook us as the railway and the road run parallel along this section. As Woking was passed, I noted that 33019, 37377, 37375, 33063 and 37274 were stabled there along with many loaded ballast wagons, ready for the night's permanent way jobs over the South Western routes. With the power on again, we soon reached 50mph on 1600amps as we ran through the heavily wooded cutting towards Brookwood. At this point I had a look around 50050. All is well, the oil pressure is 58lbs and the exhaust pipes were not overheating.

As I entered number two cab we were thundering through Winchfield at 75mph as the '50 Terminator' headed towards its first station stop at Basingstoke. There, the signalmen looked out of their box as we slowed for our stop, passing a brand new 165 turbo unit which was arriving from Reading. On time at 09.42 the horn was sounded, power was taken and the two Class 50s respond to full power. Still running under double yellows the train continued at 60mph towards Worting junction. This is a high

While 50050 and 50007 wait at London's Waterloo Station for the stock for the 50 Terminator railtour to arrive, Dicky Daw and Geoff Hudson prepare to affix the headboard. 26th March 1992. Photo: Mike Woodhouse

speed junction where the four track sections split into two double tracks, with separate routes to Southampton and Salisbury. It is at this point that we leave the third rail DC electric system.

Many photographers were spotted in the fields alongside Battledown Flyover, a well known location where we swung right under onto the Salisbury route. At Whitchurch we had reached 75mph maximum speed and as we passed through Andover station I noticed that it had been repainted and sponsored by the TSB. We were now running on jointed track and 50050 was bouncing on all the rail joints! Having run through a long chalk cutting we were nearing Salisbury where a crew change would take place. Yellow signals came into view and the speed was eased through Laverstock North junction.

Salisbury tunnel junction was then passed after which the two 50s entered the 443 yard long Fisherton tunnel. The horn sounded in the darkness and the locos headlight beam shone ahead on the rails as the line curved to the right and into the station. As we arrived, 159001 'City of Exeter' was in the next platform awaiting its next turn of duty. A crew change took place with Driver Bernie Shergold taking over for the run to Exeter. The whistle was blown by the platform staff and we departed on time at 10.17 for the next leg of the journey to Yeovil junction.

Not long after leaving Salisbury, we came to a standstill at Wilton junction to wait for an up 159 service to London Waterloo to pass as, after here, the route goes into single track. The signal then turned to green and power was taken. The locomotives wheels squealed on the rails as we made for the open Wiltshire countryside. A field of grazing sheep scuttled away as our two Class 50s thundered away at full power with horns blaring. We were soon blasting through Gillingham at 75mph as the locos thrashed their way up to Buckhorn Western tunnel.

Our driver was clearly making the most of his last time at the controls of a Class 50 and he used the horn frequently on the journey to Exeter. Two old donkeys looked up as we passed Templecombe. As we powered towards Milborne Port we passed many disused Southern Region concrete lineside huts which were made at Exmouth junction concrete works. Shortly after the summit we pass Sherborne Castle on time as we head towards Yeovil Junction. We have now covered 122 miles and it is now 11.00. The railtour comes to a stand in Yeovil Junction station where there is a booked photo stop and hundreds of enthusiasts leave the train to take their pictures in brilliant sunshine.

Tea was taken during the 25 minute break at Yeovil, after which the Pathfinder Tours stewards called everyone back onto the train. At 11.25, we are away again passing 37012 (the former 'Loch Rannoch') stabled in the sidings with a train of ballast ready for the night shift. The hot exhausts drifted by from 50050, as I was now riding on 50007. The train was now tackling the one in one hundred and fifty gradient past Sutton Bingham water reservoirs, with 50007 at 1800amps. Speed of 75mph was maintained as we passed through Crewkerne station and into the tunnel where the horn was sounded once again.

Chard junction was then passed where the lineside is dominated by its milk creamery for which millions of gallons of milk used to travel to London by train every day. Cider apple trees were dotted along the lineside and there were grey herons taking in the midday sun along the banks of the River Axe. At the site of the former Seaton junction the driver applied the brakes as we were running early. A hard pull away then takes place for the climb up Honiton bank; the crows take flight as 50050 and 50007 take full power and pound their way up to Honiton tunnel. Our driver blasts the horn in merriment, he really is enjoying himself!

I then take a look round 50007's engine room. The oil pressure at 65lbs is slightly up on 50050 as 'Sir Edward' has a newer power unit. A stop at Honiton then takes place where we pass 159021 on its way up to London from Exeter. A green signal follows and we are off again. After Whimple and Pinhoe we arrive at Exmouth junction when we are held by a red signal to allow a DMU to come off the Exmouth branch ahead of us. When the unit has cleared the section ahead of us we run down the bank through St. James Park to stop at signal E312 at Exeter Central station. Once the driver gets the green signal, the train sets off down the bank at 15mph to St. David`s, where the 50s pass to Western Region territory.

Having arrived on time, the train was then cleared of passengers before the 50s made their way to Riverside yard to run round their train. Exeter Driver Jon Morton has now taken over for the next leg of our journey and our running headcode has now changed from 1Z40 to 1Z07 - the 13.17 Exeter-Penzance. A brake test was made by the guard while the ETH supply on 50050 was switched on, as this loco was now coupled to the coaching stock. The headboard was also changed over onto 50007 as 'Sir Edward' was now leading.

An HST with power cars 43180 and 086 passed by heading west while stabled in the yard were 159003/012. A rake of stored Foster Yeoman PGA`s were stabled in Riverside yard. We drew out of the sidings and into the station for the passengers to board the train again. Newly named only hours before, Laira HST power car 43154 'INTERCITY' plus set 55 and power car 43179 'Pride of Laira' arrived into platform five to await the road back to Laira depot. Amidst all this activity, 60035 'Florence Nightingale' passed through number six road with the Saturday's only Cardiff Tidal Sidings scrap Metal train. After that, the HST set off westward.

At 13.18 the '50 Terminator' eased out of Exeter St. Davids station. Although power was opened up and our speed increased, the road ahead of us was not clear. We were brought to a stand by the old Exminster signal box to discover that the preceding HST was at a stand-still. It was quickly established that help was required so, with toolbox at the ready in my hand, my mate and I set off with our Depot Engineer to help the stricken set. Once its engines had been restarted and a power check made nothing was found to be wrong with it but it was suggested that we accompany the set to Dawlish Warren loop. If there was no further trouble we would get the railtour to pick us up. We duly assisted set 55 to Dawlish Warren loop without any sign of faults. Looking east we saw the 1Z07

The 50 Terminator railtour; taken from the Yeovil Rail Centre turntable during the scheduled Photo stop. Photo: Ian Francis

skirting the River Exe towards us, now running 20 minutes late.

Driver Morton stopped the train for us to board and I climbed onto 50050, my mate onto 50007. Rescue mission accomplished, the 1Z07 set off again for Penzance. With my ear defenders on I looked round 50050 while we ran along the banks of the River Teign estuary and through Newton Abbot. While I was in the leading cab of 50050 I looked towards my mate and AFM Geoff Hudson as we started the climb of Dainton bank through Stoneycombe. The gradients here are torturous, starting at one in ninety eight and culminating in one in forty six. I felt the train slowing and, looking down at the speedometer, I noticed a dramatic drop in the train's speed. Then I looked at the amps — nothing! Quickly turning my head, I noticed that the cooling radiator fan had stopped so I stuck my head out of the cab window and signaled to our driver (who was also wondering why the speed was dropping) that 50050 was dead.

As we were winding our way through the tight curves of the one in thirty six gradient, 50007 was doing all the work. With 50050 dead, that meant the load was equal to three and a half additional coaches — a total of thirteen and a half coaches for 50007 to haul. I dived into the engine room. The coolant and oil were ok and the engine governor had not tripped. Then I checked the electrical cubicle — all circuit breakers were in, there were no fault lights and no earth faults had tripped. On returning to the cab I wrote all the information down on paper. I then taped the paper onto the windscreen to enable my mate who was in the rear cab of 50007, to read and relay the information onto the other personnel on the footplate of 50007.

At least they knew that they had to keep 50007 powering until we reached Plymouth. Today, the whole communication exercise would have been simple thanks to mobile phones!

In days gone by we would have been able to restart 50050 en-route when coasting but all BR fleets were by then fitted with SSF (Stand Still Fitted) and therefore were only able to restart if the locomotive was at a standstill. To have attempted a restart would have resulted in an automatic brake application - and a sudden stop of the train. We passed Totnes through the station's middle road, before tackling the long drawn out climb of Rattery bank. Once again the severe curvature was the limiting factor for the next four miles. At gradients of one in forty six, 50007 was doing very well at a steady 30mph when we reached the site of the old Tigley signal box at the summit. I am still on 50050 just watching the speedometer as there is nothing else I can do whilst we are en-route — apart from listen to 'Sir Edward' pound up the bank. The 1Z07 plunged into the darkness of the single bore tunnel

at Marley Head. After a trouble free first stage of the journey, the drama has all happened since leaving Exeter and we were slowly losing time. Once we reach Plymouth though, I had no doubt that we would regain some time in Cornwall when both locomotives would be back in working order. As the 50s sped towards Hemerdon we passed the new station platforms being built at my home town of Ivybridge. Once on the down gradient it was easy work for 50007 as it coasted downhill to Plymouth station, where platform four was reached around 20 minutes late. Once the train stopped, 50050 was successfully restarted, disappointing some who had hoped that 50007 would work single handed into Cornwall.

Here, another crew change took place with Driver Mike Galvin of Plymouth taking us on to Penzance and then back to Exeter.

After 50050 was given a successful power test, the ETH button was depressed. All was well, and this was relayed to the station supervisor. With a green signal and a blow of the station whistle, power was taken and the 50s wound their way out of Plymouth and through the Devonport suburbs. In the dockyard decommissioned ships could be seen moored in the straights of the River Tamar. As we crossed the famous Royal Albert Bridge spanning the river at a steady 15mph, the tide was high and the weather was bright and sunny as we entered into Cornwall.

This magnificent bridge was Brunel`s masterpiece. Since its official opening by Prince Albert on 2nd May 1859, only relatively minor strengthening work has been required to cater for train weights far above anything known at the time of its construction. The main spans are 455 feet each in length and are 100 feet above the high water level. The whole structure, including the approach spans, is 730 yards long. We curved left through Saltash station after which the power was back on as we crossed the granite viaduct of Coombe Creek. The non-stop run from here to Penzance would enable some of the lost time over the South Devon banks to be recovered.

With both locomotives working together again, we made a steady 60mph climb up the one in sixty eight gradient of St. Germans bank. Speed was eased before the slight descent of the level section across Tresulyan and Coldrennick viaducts to Menheniot. We approached Liskeard slowly over the viaduct where a traditional GWR lower quadrant signal could be seen ahead in the 'off' position. So, with power full on, the ammeter showed 1,000 amps for the 60mph climb to Doublebois. The route ahead then singled across St. Pinnock viaduct (the highest in Cornwall at 151 feet) and East Largin viaduct. We then ran down the Glyn Valley to Lostwithiel which we passed at

55mph and on 1,600 amps before climbing at a gradient of one in fifty seven across Milltown viaduct to Treverrin tunnel. After that the route descends at one in sixty two towards Par. On arrival at Par station at 15.26 all the adjacent fields were in use for local league Saturday youth football matches. Just past the station, china clay bulk carriers were in the harbour sidings in readiness for loading on Monday morning.

Near Charlestown we slowed down to 20mph for a bridge speed restriction. Afternoon golfers and children waved as we regained power heading towards St. Austell. It was time for me to have another look round the loco and so, with ear defenders on and torch in hand, an inspection of 50007's engine room takes place. Happily, all is well. When I returned to the cab we had reached Burngullow English China Clay sidings. We were due to have stopped here to allow an up service to come off the single line to Probus but, due to our late running, we were able to continue without stopping — thus regaining several more minutes. From here we switched to single line track for the eight miles to Probus, where we regained the double track. We were now travelling at 70mph bouncing on old jointed track towards Truro.

As Truro loomed on the horizon the cathedral spires towered above the city skyline. The 50s were on full power as we ran through the station with the ammeter showing 1,900amps on the climb to Penwithers junction. The near complete Cornish mine building of Hallenbeagle, along with other mining remains, could be seen before the train entered the short 47 yard long tunnel into Redruth station. In the far distance we could see the Atlantic coast.

As the brakes are eased in I looked at my watch to discover that we were now only running 5 minutes late. The Redruth town hall clock struck 16.00 and the milepost indicated that we were 311.25 miles from London Paddington. The talk on board the loco was that we would now arrive on time at Penzance. The locos coasted through the curve at Gwinear Road before more power was taken. At Hayle the speed was eased as in the bright afternoon sunshine we caught a glimpse of the sea and the St. Ives branch line at Lelant. The power was shut off and as we coasted along, the AWS siren blew before we were brought to a stand just outside St. Erth. Thanks to some fine driving from Mike Galvin we were now 2 minutes ahead of time! We wait for the St. Ives branch DMU unit to enter the station ahead of us and then to clear the section ahead.

With the two Class 50s standing beside the GWR style signal box, Class 101 DMU L842, in Network South East livery, came off the branch, stopped in the station and then proceeded to Penzance. The lower quadrant signal then dropped to indicate a clear road ahead.

Power was taken again and with 1,900 amps showing on the ammeter, we were running on the final downhill leg to Penzance. The kettle was put on the stove for our afternoon tea as St. Michaels Mount came into view. The sea looked very inviting as we passed Marazion, where the line once again went single track for the run along the seashore and into the terminus of Penzance station. On time, we drew up to the stop blocks and shut down the two Class 50s to await the Class 08 station pilot to draw our empty stock back out of the platform and onto Long Rock depot. Hundreds of enthusiasts were everywhere, all waiting and wanting to take photographs of this momentous and final occasion. The two Class 50s were restarted under the overall roof of the station for the short light engine run out to Long Rock depot for servicing. On returning to the station, my mate and I were asked to attend to a Mark II air conditioned coach with a battery charging fault so, once the shunter had finished his duties and with the brake test done, we undertook the task of investigating the problem with the coach. The coach at fault was now behind 50007 and with the statutory safety requirements made, we were able to diagnose the fault and subsequently repair it. We now knew why 50050 'Fearless' had an engine shut down with the ETH (electric train heat) en—route over Dainton summit. The H.O.V.R (heating overload voltage relay) had operated due to the coach having a battery charging fault. If the H.O.V.R heating generator voltage exceeds the pre—determined value, this relay operates to suspend all train heating. By deenergising the train heating generator field contactor (H.F.C), this shuts down the engine via a interlock (H.F.C) at 960-980 volts and cuts off the supply to the engine run solenoid. This in turn shuts the engine down.

With Large Logo 50050 now leading, crowds gathered around the platform ends of Penzance station. The two Class 50s were now ready for the last leg of the '50 Terminator' (now headcoded as lZ50) for what would be the final Class 50 hauled train on British Rail.

Area Fleet Manager Geoff Hudson was presented with a cheque by Peter Watts of Pathfinder Tours who had sponsored the complete re-paint of 50050 'Fearless'. As the minutes to departure ticked by, the steamship 'Scillionian' had just arrived in Penzance harbour, Class 101 unit L842 left again for St. Ives and an InterCity HST pulled into the adjacent platform as it reached journeys end. Finally the big moment arrived. The signal ahead turned to green, whistles were blown, Driver Mike Galvin applied power and the train set off for London Paddington. I looked back from the rear

After the tour 50050 and 50007 ran light engine from Reading to Laira, where the team (L-R: Nick Edwards Andy Snowden, Dicky Daw, Malcolm Wishart and Geoff Hudson) are captured to mark the end of the BR class 50 era. Photo: Mike Woodhouse

cab of 50050 across Penzance harbour to see the sun setting behind the station clock tower after a beautiful day. We were to retrace our steps back towards Plymouth but, by the time we reached the Tamar estuary, darkness had fallen. At Saltash we came to a halt to await the passing of a HST service which was crossing the single track bridge.

Once that had passed, the 50s eased the train onto Brunel's famous bridge which was partially illuminated by the beautiful moonlit night. The coach lights could be seen reflecting in the water below and as the signal ahead cleared to green, both Class 50s responded to power to take us back into Devon and into Plymouth station at 19.16. The station was full of atmosphere for the last British Rail Class 50-hauled train. Even ex—Laira driving staff made an appearance; also many locals turned up with their video cameras to record the historic event. For ten minutes, the platform was alive with people saying "Farewell" to this popular locomotive Class that had brought faster journey times to the West Country before the advent of the HST's. With everyone back on board, the journey to London Paddington is underway again. Not far out of Plymouth a 20mph speed restriction over the bridge at Plympton will make our pair of 50s bark when they start to climb Hemerdon bank with its fearsome one in forty two gradient. With the restriction speed cleared 5,400hp was at full tilt on the climb. The speedometer was dropping back although 40 mph was maintained at 1,600 amps. On this moonlit night I could see the silhouette of

50007's cab in the cab window of 50050 in front of me. This was quite spooky in the darkness as the two 50s thundered over the summit.

As I undertook an engine room inspection on 50050 a comment was made that, if the leading coach tripped again, it would be 50007's turn to shut down this time. Exeter was reached without incident and a final crew change was made. Andy Snowden and Traction Inspector Nick Edwards boarded 'Fearless' for the remainder of the journey to London and would return with us on the light engine move back to Laira depot the following day. The road barriers at Exeter closed and the 1Z50 set off on its final journey. As London Paddington drew nearer, somehow I could not believe that this was the end of the Class 50s in British Rail service. As Taunton and Westbury were passed a welcome cup of tea was taken en—route.

After more good running, Reading was reached three minutes early at 22.35. Not far to go now! On this very final leg of the journey, the horns were sounded as the two 50s powered out of Reading station where we crossed over from the up relief line to the up fast line. A spirited run then took place along the Thames Valley to London through Maidenhead and Slough.

By the time we reached Southall we were running on yellow signals before coming to an eventual stop outside Old Oak Common depot. All that remained were the last three miles into London Paddington station. On the other side of the main line was the new EPS (European Passenger Services) depot at North Pole where 73139 and 73140 were stabled. A little delayed, the 50s powered up for the last time to run on caution signals. We entered London Paddington station with a fanfare of horns to mark the end and I could hear the echoes coming back from the massive overall roof. Large crowds were waiting to greet us and we finally came to rest on number ten platform stop blocks at 23.40. What a truly wonderful sight to behold!

Finally the end had come. Handshakes, smiles, somber weeping faces were all observed.

What an occasion to be part of. The wreath that was placed on the front of 50050 'Fearless' said it all.

Workings: Class 50 Mileages 1992–1994		Mileage	Mileage	Mileage
Date	Workings	50007	50033	D400
25/1/1992	Pathfinder Tours: **Network Navigator** Birmingham, Fratton, Portsmouth, Littlehampton, Bognor Regis, +50030 Light Engine: Laira, Birmingham, Laira			452.59 435.06
1/2/1992	S.E.G. Tours: **Meldon Hoover** Clapham, Salisbury, Bristol, Exeter, Meldon Quarry, Salisbury, Waterloo. Light Engine: Laira, Waterloo, Laira		327.15 694.00	
4/4/1992	Pathfinder Tours: **Hoovering Druid** Derby, Pontycymer, Ebbw Vale, Newport, Derby Light Engine: Laira, Derby, Laira	400.75 517.44	400.75 517.44	
11/4/1992	Rail Magazine: **Carlisle Fifty Farewell** Waterloo-Carlisle-Waterloo Light engine Laira, Waterloo, Laira	683.48 448.30		683.48 448.30
16/5/1992	Punshanger: **Chiltern Atmospheric 50s** Aylesbury, Plymouth, Gloucester, Aylesbury Light engine: Laira, OOC, Aylesbury, OOC, Laira	260.78 263.55	309.01 263.55	569.79 527.30
23/5/1992	NSE: 14.22 Exeter, Basingstoke Light engine Laira ,Exeter 52.00 Light engine: Basingstoke, Westbury, Laira		114.31 52.00 128.30	
24/5/1992	NSE: 09.20 Exeter, Basingstoke 10.55 Ex Waterloo, Exeter 15.43 Exeter, Salisbury 16.55 Ex Waterloo, Exeter Light engine: Laira, Exeter, Laira	88.49 88.49 88.49 88.49 104.06		88.49 88.49 88.49 88.49 104.06
13/6/1992	SRR/TV50G: **Court Chester** Waterlo0, Chester , London St. Pancras Light engine Laira, Waterloo, St. Pancras, Laira	519.48 465.00		519.48 465.00
28/6/1992	NSE: Steam/Diesel Special ECS Laira, Waterloo Waterloo, Salisbury Salisbury, Waterloo Waterloo, Laira	347.00 83.00 83.00 347.00		347.00 83.00 83.00 347.00
5/7/1992	Taunton 150: Light engine: Laira, Bishops Lydeard, Laira	171.70		171.70
6/7/1992	Trial run: Laira, Bristol, Laira		254.00	
20/9/1992	Thornaby Open Day: Light engine: Laira, Thornaby, Laira			794.00
27/9/1992	Eastleigh Open Day: Laira, Eastleigh, Laira			408.00
7/11/1992	Pathfinder Tours: **Minster Marauder** Bristol, York, Bristol Light engine: Laira, Bristol, Laira	568.54 245.18	568.54 245.18	
5/12/1992	Class Forty Appeal: **Festive Fifties** Nuneaton, Llandudno Junction, Blaenau Ffestiniog, Holyhead, Nuneaton Light engine: Laira, Nuneaton, Laira		412.28 477.06	412.28 477.06
22&23& 24/1/1993	Pathfinder Tours: **Knighton Horse** Gloucester, Central Wales Line, Shrewsbury, G1oucester Light engine: Laira, Gloucester, Laira	347.23 333.00		347.23 333.00
24&25 &26/4/1993	Mid Hants Railway Light engine: Laira, Alton 8 trips between Alton and Alresford	204.00 88.88	204.00 88.88	
2/5/1993	Light engine: Alton, Old Oak Common Worcester Openday: Light engine: Old Oak Common, Worcester, Laira	76.00 343.00	76.00 343.00	
31/5/1993	Class 40 Appeal: **The Cornishman** Exeter, Plymouth, Penzance, Bristol Light engine: Laira, Exeter, and Bristol, Laira	286.52 127.49	179.52 179.52	179.52 179.52
5/6/1993	Pathfinder Tours: **Bishops Triple** Bishops Lydeard, York, Bishops Lydeard Light engine: Laira—Bishops Lydeard-Laira	258.77 85.75	517.64 171.70	517.64 171.70
28/6/1993	F.F.S./NSE: Waterloo, Eastleigh, Waterloo Light engine: Laira, Waterloo, Laira	146.70 448.30		146.70 448.30
18/7/1993	Hertfordshire Railtours: **Atlantic Coast Express** Waterloo, Barnstaple, Exmouth, Exeter, Waterloo Light engine: Laira, WIaterloo, Laira		222.46 52.00	394.58 448.30
30/8/1993	Pathfinder Tours: **North Yorkshireman**: 50007 at York—for return to Laira York, Leeds, York: for Fuel York, Reading Light Engine: Reading, Laira	80 235.07 189.57		

		50007	50033	D400
5/9/1993	NSE: Waterloo, Exeter	172.12		172.12
	Light engine: Laira, Waterloo	224.15		224.15
	Intercity: Exeter, Plymouth	52.03		52.03
9/9/21993	Intercity: Plymouth, Newport, Plymouth	308.61		308.61
25/9/1993	Intercity: Plymouth, Meldon Quarry, Plymouth		157.40	157.40
26/9/1993	Intercity: Plymouth, Penzance, Plymouth	159.04	159.04	
16/10/1993	Light engine: Laira, Paddington	245.75	245.75	
	Intercity: Paddington, Paignton	201.53	**307.33**	
	Light engine: Plymouth, Paignton			39.00
	Paignton, Reading			165.60
	Paignton, Kingswear shuttles	39.42	26.28	26.28
	Paignton, Paddington		245.75	245.75
	Light engine: Paignton, Plymouth	39.00		
17/10/1993	Light engine: Reading, Westbury, Laira		189.57	189.57
31/10/1993	Pathfinder Tours: **Merseyman**			
	Light engine: Laira, Bristol	122.49	122.49	
	Bristol, Edge Hill, Bristol	434.73	434.73	
	Light engine: Bristol, Laira	122.49	122.49	
8/1/1994	Pathfinder Tours: **Dyfed Dub-Dub**			
	Crewe, Fishguard Harbour, Crewe	635.00	635.00	
5/2/1994	Class Forty Appeal: **The Midland Scotsman**			
	Light engine: Laira, Saltley, Oxley		236.16	236.16
	ECS: Oxley, Birmingham		19.03	19.03
	Birmingham—Glasgow via the Settle and Carlisle		328.08	328.08
	Light engine: Glasgow, Motherwell, Glasgow		25.82	25.82
	Glasgow, Birmingham		288.00	288.00
	ECS: Birmingham, Oxley		19.03	19.03
	Light engine: Oxley, Saltley, Laira		236.16	236.16
19/2/1994	Class Forty Appeal: **Western Memorial**			
	Light engine: Laira, Crewe	263.05	263.05	
	Crewe, Paddington, Exeter (terminated at Exeter due to late running)	380.06	380.06	
	Exeter, Crewe	319.84	319.84	
	Light engine: Crewe, Saltley, Laira	270.51	270.51	
18-19/3/1994	Pathfinder Tours: **Cornish Caper**			
	Light engine: Laira, Bristol		122.49	122.49
	Bristol, Plymouth		122.49	122.49
	Plymouth, Newquay	55.42	55.42	55.42
	Newquay, Par	20.43	20.43	20.43
	Par, Penzance	44.61	44.61	44.61
	Penzance, St Ives, Penzance	20.18	20.18	20.18
	Penzance, Plymouth	79.42	79.42	79.42
	Plymouth, York		425.68	425.68
20/3/1994	Pathfinder Tours: **The Glorious Sunset**			
	York, Scarborough, York		84.12	
	Light engine: York, Laira			346.26
25-28/3/1994	Pathfinder Tours: **50 Terminator**			
	Light engine: Laira, Stewarts Lane, Waterloo	224.15		224.15
	Waterloo, Penzance, Paddington	608.74		608.74
	Light engine: Paddington, Laira	244.00		244.00

Overall Mileages 1992-1994

		50007	50033	D400
	1992	5804.03	4867.57	9564.65
	1993	5205.21	4045.55	4580.60
	1994	1931.95	3493.08	5589.60

FURTHER WOODHOUSE WANDERINGS

1: Bodmin and Wenford Railway: 50042 'Triumph' — March 1996

Martin Blackwell of the Bodmin and Wenford Railway contacted me at home for advice and help with the removal of 50042's number two bogie as number six traction motor had gone to earth.

This is preservation in the raw, to lift 50042 outside in the station yard on sleepers, to pack and jack it by hand using hydraulic jacks. This was no mean feat

— what a challenge!

This is not Laira on a flat concrete base in a warm shed with electrically operated synchronized jacks so it was a sharp learning curve for me. But safety had to be paramount!

It was suggested that both bogies be disconnected to make it stable and safer for lifting.

Over the next week or so, 50042 'Triumph' had its traction motors, air pipes, safety chains, speedometer drive, earth cables and traction motor bellows disconnected in readiness for the lift.

The Fifty Fund let the Bodmin Railway borrow their Class 50 lifting brackets and these were fitted into the four outer corners on 50042.

The Class 08 diesel electric shunting locomotive placed 50042 in Bodmin General station yard ready for its jacking.

Many sleepers along with elm wood packing were placed on the uneven terrain under the four lifting corners.

I made my way down to the Bodmin and Wenford Railway in March 1996 to help with the final removal of 50042`s number two bogie. Inch by inch 50042 was hand jacked into the air end by end. Once the maximum height was reached more packing had to be added.

Finally 50042`s number two bogie was clear of the centre pivot. But there was a small snag — the bottom packing had slightly moved during the jacking process. To remove the bogie we had to remove number ten brake cylinder. Once this was done the Class 08 diesel shunter, which had steel chains attached to it, slowly pulled the bogie out from under 50042.

More elm wood packing was added over number one bogie bolster so that 50042 could rest safely overnight. Number two bogie was removed to the steam shed and positioned over the pit. The steam operated crane had built up pressure, having been lit up in the early hours.

Meanwhile we made ready number six traction motor for removal from the axle suspension.

Tea and Cornish pasties were taken — what else could you have in Cornwall?!

By now a full head of steam pressure had been raised on the crane which now had its safety valves lifted.

After removal of the axle bearings we lifted out the old 'down to earth' number six traction motor. The axle cannon tube was examined, the fibre shells are greased and are then put back on the axle to await refitting.

Mid-afternoon the steam crane swings into action once more, lifting the new traction motor into place. We refit all the components and secured the number six traction motor into place. A check was made on the overhauled unit with electrical tests and meggering being done to check the electrical insulation resistance before the bogie is returned to 50042. The class 08 shunter then towed the bogie back to 50042, stopping just short of the nose end. A gang of helpers hand push the number two bogie slowly underneath the locomotive to realign the bogie pivot. Packing was then added across the bogie bolster so that 50042 could rest overnight. Saturday was closing in on us but what an achievement in preservation as the task had been accomplished without the need for a major depot.

At dawn on Sunday morning 50042 is still as we left it — up in the air and still on packing. Slowly in reverse order 'Triumph' was lowered each end, evenly attaching the traction motor bellows as we went, until the loco was resting back onto its bogies ready for all the other re-connections to be made. The borrowed lifting brackets were then removed from the four corners so that they could be returned by road back to The Fifty Fund at a later date.

So, well done to all, 50042 'Triumph' was now back to full working order on her home ground at the Bodmin and Wenford Railway.

2: North York Moors Railway: 50027 'Lion' - 23 April 1999

I was invited by the owner of 50027 'Lion', Mike Fuller, to go to the North Yorkshire Moors Railway with my friend and former Laira colleague, Dicky Daw, for a working and riding weekend.

The 06.25 Plymouth-Newcastle Cross Country HST was taken to York where we were met by Mike at 12.40. We were then ferried across the North Yorkshire Moors to Grosmont station where we took refreshments in the buffet.

We made our way through the tunnel footpath leading to the running shed where we shook hands with the on duty supervisor before greeting the members of the 'Lion' support group. There was a known speedometer fault which needed to be investigated. 'Lion' was started up so that the main reservoir air pressure could build up. A driver was sourced for the loco to move in the sidings so that the fault could be diagnosed. It was found that number two cab speedometer gauge was faulty. Trains were running, mainly steam, these being 80135, 75029, with Mark I and LNER teak coaching stock.

West Country Class re-build 34101 'Hartland' was on the shed being pre-heated for the next day's duty (Saturday). We decided to remove the speedometer gauge from the desk of 'Lion' to see if it could be repaired. Meanwhile the others were doing duties in and around 50027 'Lion'.

It looked like the gauge resistance windings were burnt so Dicky decided to unwind and count the turns. He soon came across the break.

A soldering iron and solder were required to fuse the copper wire together and this was done via the workshop. It was now early evening and it had been a long day. After the repair had been made we left the number two gauge in the cab to await fitting the following morning.

We had all had a very tiring day and what we needed most was food, drink and a good night's sleep ready for tomorrow. So a drive to the village of Egton for an evening supper at 'Ye Horseshoe Inn' was in order. Stories of Class 50`s at Laira were told during a very pleasant evening before we retired to our bed and breakfast at the hotel. The whole support group and ourselves stayed with George at Grosmont House which overlooked the station. At breakfast there were more tales of railway work at Laira, after which it was back to Grosmont running shed to rejoin 50027 'Lion'. We were given the news that 50027 would be required to run at lunchtime, to make two trips from Grosmont to Pickering. The speedometer head was replaced while 'Lion', in Network SouthEast livery (the only 50 now in those colours. **Update:** several others have since carried variations of the NSE livery), was fully serviced ready for its afternoon and evening outings.

A very memorable couple of trips were made over the beautiful North Yorkshire Moors Railway, with its heathers and gorses seen in all their glory. The speedometer at number two end was now reading and the driver commented that 'its higher than number one end'.

A good look around the engine room and the generator was made while the loco was under power — it was just like the old days. It was now getting late and by the time we got back to Grosmont shed and had put 'Lion' to bed, we missed a quick night drink at the local, so instead we returned to Grosmont House for our nightcap. Sunday after breakfast we headed back to the locomotive shed where we sheeted 50027 'Lion' over until her next turns of duty. Mike Fuller drove Dicky and myself back to York station to catch the 13.00 York—Plymouth H.S.T (ex-Edinburgh) back to Devon.

And so, another Woodhouse Wandering story draws to a close following a very enjoyable and satisfying weekend.

3: Plym Valley Railway: 50017 'Royal Oak' — March 2010

Just after the New Year passed into 2010 a telephone call came to my home in Ivybridge from a friend who I have not seen since the '50 Terminator' railtour of 1994.

I was asked to make contact with the new owner of 50017 'Royal Oak', Dave Cunningham, who needed advice about the locomotive being based on the Plym Valley Railway at Plympton. This was only a few miles from the locomotive's old home of Laira depot, in Plymouth. This I duly did.

'Royal Oak' has had a very chequered history. I researched the loco from D417 from new to its current status. History showed that 50017 'Royal Oak' had a very varied career over its years on the London Midland Region and the Western Region of British Rail. The new weight transfer equipment was fitted from new to this locomotive (the only one to have that done) and it was the first of its

Class to be painted into Network SouthEast livery at Laira depot in 1986.

Arrangements were made for me to meet Dave at the Plym Valley Railway and I was greeted warmly by him and Chairman John Netherton. We walked over to the siding where 50017 'Royal Oak' was stabled and climbed aboard into number two cab. Dave explained that 50017 had arrived as a running locomotive. It had run and was powered once since its arrival on 9th June 2009. I remarked that I had followed it down the A38 when it was moved by Heanor Heavy Haulage Transport on that particular day.

Like all other locomotives that are forty years old, some new plating was required around the cab areas and this will be done in the course of time. Once all the body side repairs are completed a full re-paint into a yet-to—be-decided livery will then take place.

We both made a thorough examination of 50017 and I gave him some guidance on keeping 'Royal Oak' operational while maintaining the locomotives electrics and mechanics in order to keep it running. At this time my main interest focused on 50017`s power unit (number IH6933) particularly its timing chain which, if it failed, would be extremely costly to repair.

On my next visit we set about checking the timing chain and this was done within an hour. I found the timing chain to be in tolerance so there was a big sigh of relief as the engine could start safely.

In March 2010 a small group of enthusiasts came for a visit, via 73133 in the Colas yard at Tavistock junction, then to see 50017 at its new preserved home. After all the body side tarpaulins had been removed, the power unit was barred over. With all the de-compressors open there were no signs of water or coolant in any of the cylinders. So that was good news. With the battery switch now live we turned the engine over before closing all the de-compressors.

Having primed the oil and fuel systems the start button was duly depressed and 50017 burst into life, building up air pressure as it did so. The power unit was smoky but it cleared within ten minutes to a light blue haze.

Power was tested from each cab and the loco moved up and down the siding within the PVR complex to the great enjoyment of all those present. One guest, Phillip Seymore, who was about to be married and had arranged with the PVR for a private charter using 50017. The loco was still carrying the 1930`s LMS crimson lake livery which had been applied in 2000 when the locomotive was intended to be used as a train heat locomotive 'Thunderbird' when running with streamlined 6229 'Duchess of Hamilton'. That never came to fruition and the project was abandoned.

50017 'Royal Oak' in the striking Network SouthEast livery (with white wheel detailing) on the Plym Valley Railway. Photo: Matt Veale

Easter Saturday 3rd April and 50017 'Royal Oak' was masquerading as 50012 'Benbow' (Phillip's favourite Class 50), and it was used for the private stag charter. This was something he knew nothing about so it was a big surprise for him on the day. Having been asked to attend by the owner, I assisted on the loco on the day. I had not been on a Class 50 since 50027 'Lion' in the early days of preservation in 1999. But hey -here is yet another challenge!

From a professional point of view, there was to be no risk and no failure as we had to demonstrate to the committee of the PVR that a Class 50 would be of benefit to 'The Woodland Line'.

With spectacular majesty, 'Royal Oak/Benbow' ran faultlessly, towing the Class 117 diesel multiple unit on four round trips of the Plym Valley Railway. All the organisers were delighted with the 'Stag `n Oak' private charter and a good party was really enjoyed by all.

Cornish pasties, ale and the traditional ceremonial cake were consumed by all present. This was the largest locomotive to work over the ex-Great Western branch line from Tavistock to Plymouth. Future excursions should keep 50017 'Royal Oak' a working locomotive in the years to come.

By the late Autumn of 2010 50017 `Royal Oak` had the full body restoration commenced which was started in the yard before entry into the shed over the winter period, where work then continued. First signs of the progress appeared in late January when the first layer of green rust proofing

undercoat appeared. Generally it was then discovered there was a lot more welding work required than originally thought, the locomotive was therefore allowed to continue under cover for further weeks whilst being made watertight.

By the spring of 2012 Class Fifty 50017 `Royal Oak`s` restoration was completed after nearly twenty months. Dave and his small team had created a locomotive which had the finish and quality of professional workmanship all of which everybody was rightly very proud of. Many people have passed comments either verbally or via the internet saying how fantastic the locomotive looked being in the original Network South East livery as it did back in 1986 at the launch of that Company under British Rail.

People were convinced that the locomotive was spray painted and not hand painted, this was true testament to the hundreds even thousands of hours from all the dedicated volunteering team who together had made such a fantastic job.

Finally by April 50017 `Royal Oak` was to enter service on the Plym Valley Railway, the `Woodland Line`.

On the 5 May 50017 `Royal Oak` was re-dedicated which was a very moving experience for me and the witnesses looking on. The ceremony was carried out by a ships Crewe member Kenneth Toop aged 91 who survived the sinking of the ship `Royal Oak`.

At the outbreak of the Second World War the Devonport based Battleship `Royal Oak` was torpedoed and sunk with the loss of some 834 lives in Scapa Flow off the Orkney Isles, Scotland in the early hours of 14 October 1939, the first ship sunk of WWII. With a tear in his eye Kenneth Toop recorded how the name of `Royal Oak` came about and read out a prayer for all his lost comrades from that terrible night. Mr Toop praised Dave Cunningham for the work done on restoring 50017 and making such a fantastic job. The whole event was supported by the Royal British Legion Association with all enjoying a trip up the line making this ceremonial occasion complete.

Class fifty 50017 `Royal Oak` saw Sunday workings in August that year followed by `Spooky Sunday` of Halloween.

After some fifty years of closure and thirty years of the Plym Valley Railway on 30 December 2012 the end of the line at Plymbridge platform was reached and re-opened. The trains were packed with VIP`s and guests, steam hauled running until the last two trains of the day, when Class 50017 `Royal Oak` was used for these last two trips. What a great day for this locomotive as part of the celebrations 50017 had passed the `Worlds End` en route

By now Dave was fully aware that 50017 was always no more from a press of a button away from a failure, it being 44 years old and would need some very deep pockets if a main generator or traction motors were to "go to earth".

For myself, it was time to step back as we had all had fun with 50017 within the last five years.

In 2014 Dave Cunningham sold 'Royal Oak' onto Neil Boden in Birmingham, 50017`s next chapter started on being winched onto a low loader for its trip up the M5 Motorway onto its new home.

Today in March 2021 Dave Cunningham is now a proud owner of a Class 31, 31190 for a new saga to begin on the Plym Valley Railway but at the time this was originally written he had yet to take delivery. That delivery was completed on 6th April 2021.

As to 50017, it spent several years plying its trade back on the main line with 50050 and 50007, before Neil's fleet was reduced. 50007 'Hercules' was the first to go when it was sold to The Class 50 Alliance, and then 50017 'Royal Oak', which was purchased by new owners who have based it on the Great Central Railway.

In Conclusion

My railway career spanned nearly 40 years, during which time I have had the great pleasure and privilege of working on the Class 50s.

Having produced this and the previous books, I sincerely hope that you have had an enjoyable and enlightening read and understand the ups and downs of working on these difficult and frustrating machines.

Kind regards

Mike Woodhouse

2010

50008 'Thunderer', 50015 'Valiant' and 50031 'Hood' in their celebrity liveries stand outside Laira Depot as part of the display for the open day on 15th September 1991. Photo: Carl Looker

The Fifty Fund

The Fund was formed in the late 1980s with the aim of buying, preserving and operating at least one class 50 locomotive. Over the period of the class run down by British Rail, the Fund were successful in acquiring three locomotives, along with a good collection of spare parts. A few years later The Fifty Fund merged with Project Defiance Ltd, creating The Class 50 Alliance Ltd to own and operate the combined fleet four locomotives. The Fifty Fund was then reformed as a mutual society, to undertake publicity, education and fund raising activities. Since then, two further locomotives have become our responsibility; one purchased by the Alliance, and a second loaned to us by The Tyseley Locomotive Works. Our fleet now comprises: 50007 *Hercules*, 50031 *Hood*, 50033 *Glorious*, 50035 *Ark Royal*, 50044 *Exeter*, and 50049 *Defiance*.

Most of the locomotive maintenance work is undertaken by volunteers at our Kidderminster base on the Severn Valley Railway. Here the locos are regularly operated on public services, and the mainline connection also allows our locos to readily attend events on other preserved railways.

50007, 50044 and 50049 are currently registered to operate on the national railway network under their own power, and therefore can be seen on excursion trains and stock moves. To secure their future, all the revenue generated by these operations and the sale of this book and other railway memorabilia is ploughed back into our locomotives.

You too can join, by purchasing a share in the Class 50 Alliance, details can be found on our website: This year, 2022, is the twenty fifth anniversary of our first mainline operation (the Pilgrim Hoover), and the thirtieth first anniversary of the purchase of the first of those locomotives for preservation, an exercise that has been supported by Mike throughout. We extend our thanks to him for his efforts and for agreeing to let us publish these reminiscences.

Fifty Fund volunteers remove the diesel set and main generator from 50033 'Glorious' at our operating base at the Kidderminster Diesel Depot on 12th June 2021. Photo: Dan Holmes

The Fifty Fund
www.fiftyfund.org.uk

50035 Ark Royal

50044 Exeter

50031 Hood

50049 Defiance

50007 Hercules

50033 Glorious